THE WORLD'S WORST
HISTORICAL DISASTERS

THE WORLD'S WORST
HISTORICAL DISASTERS

CHRONICLING THE GREATEST CATASTROPHES OF ALL TIME

CHRIS McNAB

BARNES & NOBLE BOOKS

NEW YORK

CONTENTS

INTRODUCTION

RECENT, APPALLING EVENTS IN THE INDIAN OCEAN HAVE REMINDED US HOW FRAGILE HUMAN BEINGS ARE UNDER THE POWERS OF NATURE, AND HOW ABRUPTLY AN ENTIRE WORLD REGION CAN GO FROM NORMALITY TO CATASTROPHE.

In the Western world, in particular, the comforting wrap of our relatively prosperous lives shields us from an uncomfortable historical truth – major disasters are common, recurrent features in almost every generation. Whether the disasters are caused by geological events, by social causes (war, riot etc.) or by industrial or mechanical accident, they cast a perpetual shadow.

NATURAL DISASTERS
In terms of sheer death toll, natural disasters have undoubtedly shown themselves as the most powerful calamities, rivalled only in death tolls by some of the world's largest wars. Natural disasters can be climatological, such as hurricanes, tornadoes, blizzards and flood; be geological, including earthquakes, volcanoes and landslides; or originate in famine and disease. When of sufficient magnitude, natural disasters often produce effects far beyond the immediate area they strike. The most famous volcanic eruption

in history, that of Krakatoa on 27 August 1883, not only exploded with a force many times greater than that of the largest nuclear weapon tested on earth, but also raised a tsunami that struck the coastline of what is today Indonesia and killed 36,000 people. Such were the quantities of volcanic ash that Krakatoa ejected into the atmosphere, global temperatures dipped by more than 1°C (34°F).

HIGH DEATH TOLLS

As Krakatoa illustrates, the death tolls from violent natural events can be terrifyingly large. In 856, for example, an earthquake at the ancient city of Corinth killed an estimated 45,000 people in only a few seconds of tremors. Nor is such a death toll unusual. Even in the modern world earthquakes have catastrophic consequences – the earthquake in the Iranian city of Bam in 2003 killed 26,000 people, although many deaths occurred because housing was of traditional, fragile mud-brick and palm-trunk construction.

Yet if we were to talk crudely about the 'worst' type of natural disaster, those involving flooding seem to generate disproportionately high death tolls. The final death toll of the Indian Ocean tsunami is likely to remain for ever unknown, but it has reached somewhere in the region of 300,000 fatalities. There are equally dreadful

➤➤

precedents. In 1970 an estimated half a million people died from storm flooding when a massive cyclone hit Bangladesh. An unfortunate pattern emerges from studying many natural disasters – those countries with high rates of poverty usually suffer from the greatest death tolls, as the housing structures and medical systems are ill equipped to cope with destructive physical events. In this light it is revealing that while 26,000 people died in Bam in 2003, 'only' 3000 died in the massive San Francisco earthquake back in 1908, most of the destruction from the latter event coming from subsequent fire rather than the tremors. In addition, while we identify a disaster with the exploding volcano or raging hurricane, for example, the twin destroyers, famine and disease, often compound that event in the aftermath.

FAMINE AND DISEASE

Of all the killers throughout human history, none approaches the sheer lethal effects of famine and disease. Often the two have followed in the wake of an initial disaster. There are numerous example of this, in 1931, for example, the Yellow River and several other major river systems in China broke their banks after torrential rains. A total of around 140,000 people alone died in the flooding, but a breathtaking 3.6 million subsequently died from famine and disease. Flooding carries particularly high risks of bringing long-term mortality in its wake, via several mechanisms. First of all sewerage and drinking-water systems are often mixed during floods, facilitating the spread of diseases such as cholera. Cholera results in rapid dehydration, and with the drinking water contaminated the affected people cannot implement the rehydration required to recover. The dead then further complicate the issue, corpses decomposing in the water systems also accelerate the spread of disease. The famine component of flooding disasters comes quite simply from ruined crops, but there is an added blow delivered by flooding from the sea. The salt deposits left by evaporated seawater are ruinous to fields for many years – in the early centuries the Romans used to sow enemy fields with salt as an act of war.

Of course, famine and disease do not need an inundation to take hold. Drought can precipitate awful famines, as the continent of Africa regularly experiences, and even human interference has caused horrific famine disasters. Between 1959 and 1961 China suffered one of the worst famines known in all history, largely through the implementation of insane communist agricultural policies that overplanted fields, destroyed much of the bird population (this consequently encouraged a population boom in plant-eating insects) and prohibited the use of all fertilizers. The awful result of these policies was that an estimated 30–40 million people died of starvation, this was a terrible crime surpassing even the manmade famines created by Stalin during the 1930s.

➤

Like famines, diseases are often not treated as disasters unless they reach newsworthy magnitude. Diseases emerge slowly, over wide areas, and last for many years, even centuries. Such a development does not have the immediacy we associate with natural disasters, and yet diseases have proved to be among the most profound human calamities. Probably the greatest of all human disasters has been disease-related – during the Black Death of 1348–51, the entire society of Europe was brought to the very edge of collapse by an epidemic that killed 75 million people, one-third of the continent's population.

MEDICAL UNDERSTANDING

Looking so far back in history, we might be consoled that such a horror could never be visited on the modern world, with its immeasurably greater medical understanding. Yet the confidence is unfortunately misplaced. Early in the twentieth century, the influenza pandemic of 1918–19 killed an astonishing amount of people, around 70 million worldwide, despite there being good awareness of the methods of disease transmission. More recently, estimates of HIV/AIDS deaths in Africa alone have been projected at around 90 million by 2025. Even largely ignored tropical diseases such as malaria kill one million people every year. From such a perspective, natural disasters are not something which visits the human world every now and then, but phenomena which constantly roll on in different forms year on year and often result in unimaginable havoc and numerous horrendous deaths.

SOCIAL AND TECHNOLOGICAL DISASTERS

In many ways we are largely powerless to resist natural disasters, aside from preventative measures and effective disaster-response systems. Yet every year there are disasters caused by humankind itself, either through negligence or mechanical failure, or through wilful destruction. There is a loose historical pattern to major disasters of this type. Prior to the industrial revolution of the eighteenth and nineteenth centuries, the primary vehicle for urban disasters caused by human beings was fire. The Great Fire of Rome in AD 64 broke out among the shopping stalls of the Circus Maximus and ended up gutting 10 of Rome's 14 districts. Six hundred years later, London was devastated by a fire which destroyed 150 hectares (373 acres) of the city and more than 13,000 houses.

To this day, fire persists as a major cause of urban death, alongside other age-old social calamities such as riot and building collapse. Nonetheless the increasing presence of technological innovations, particularly in terms of travel, from the early 1800s has brought a whole new world of tragic potential alongside fresh liberties and benefits. Trains, airships, fixed-wing aircraft, high-rise buildings, spaceships,

➤➔

industrial manufacture – all have added to the variety of disaster that interrupts normal life. When such disasters occur, they do not have the gross death tolls that come with natural disasters, but on a localized scale they are just as hideous. The Bhopal gas disaster of 1984 has killed 20,000 people to date and has resulted in tens of thousands of birth defects and other health disorders. On occasions the number of fatalities is very small, but the poignant circumstances of the accident make the disaster worthy of such a title – the loss of the space shuttle Columbia in 2003 is one such example.

MANMADE DISASTERS

Human beings live in a world of risk, and as such accidental and natural disasters are part and parcel of the fabric of our existence, although that recognition makes them no less tragic when they occur. Far harder to rationalize are those disasters caused by intentional human agency. The 3000 people who died in the September 11, 2001, attacks in the United States were part of a conscious desire to precipitate disaster –

that the death toll probably exceeded the terrorists' intentions would have caused their leaders only increased satisfaction. The *Wilhelm Gustloff* horror which was a German transport ship torpedoed in the Baltic in 1945 with the loss of nearly 9500 people – took place within history's largest manmade disaster, World War II. During this six-year conflict an estimated 56 million people were killed, including 25 million. Soviet citizens, 10 million Chinese and 6 million Jews. This global catastrophe can be traced back to the actions of just one or two people, something which attests to humankind's vulnerability before powerful individuals. Instances of deliberate disaster creation are included in this book, but they are relatively few and serve more to highlight the fact that conscious decision can be just as dangerous as negligence or nature.

The disasters charted here can make for grim reading, yet there is a chink of light. Humanity is still here and thriving, despite millennia of earthquakes, tornadoes, asteroid strikes, fires, tsunami and pandemics. Viewed as such, disasters are as much a testimony to human durability as they are to human vulnerability.

ANCIENT DISASTERS
3000 BC – AD 1

Disasters loom large in the earliest recorded histories of humankind. By only the sixth book of Genesis in the Judaeo-Christian scriptures, the writer gives account of a great flood that wipes out all people except those whom God permits to be saved. Other early religious writings contain similar disaster traditions. Apart from the perennial visitations from forces of war, the ancient world suffered predominantly from natural disasters, particularly earthquakes, volcanoes, tsunami and disease. There is no doubt a catalogue of other contemporary disasters hidden from historical record, with the subsistence lifestyle of many ancient peoples leaving them very exposed to famine.

Left: The Cretan Tsunami created by a huge volcanic explosion on the Aegean island of Thera.

SODOM AND GOMORRAH

POSSIBLY ONE OF THE EARLIEST RECORDED DISASTERS IS BIBLICAL, AND IS DESCRIBED IN GENESIS CHAPTER 19.

Here, in the first book of the Old Testament, is recounted the admonitory tale of the cities of Sodom and Gomorrah.

DESTROYED BY GOD

In the biblical story, God, finding that there is no one without sin in the two cities, obliterates both from the face of the earth. Only Lot and his wife are allowed to flee, the latter being turned to a pillar of salt when she turns back to gaze on the destruction. The language is vivid: 'Then the Lord rained down burning sulphur on Sodom and Gomorrah – from the Lord out of the heavens. Thus he overthrew those cities and the entire plain, including all those living in the cities – and also the vegetation in the land.'

In recent years, scientists and historical geologists have begun to unpack the reality behind the biblical legend, and have discovered new evidence not only that Sodom and Gomorrah existed, but also that they were indeed destroyed in the early Bronze Age, around 2350 BC. The actual location of the cities has been plausibly ➤➤

KEY FACTS

Destruction of Sodom and Gomorrah recounted in Genesis 19.

Evidence suggests that an earthquake occurred around the Dead Sea, the likeliest area of location for Sodom and Gomorrah, c.2380 BC.

The earthquake could have caused major landslides and large deposits of sulphurous bitumen to fall from the sky.

The destruction of Sodom and Gomorrah has been depicted throughout history as the archetypal example of divine wrath.

Above: In the biblical tale of Sodom and Gomorrah, Lot's wife was warned by angels not to look back upon the destruction of the cities. She ignored the divine advice, and as a punishment was transformed into a pillar of salt.

pinpointed through archaeological evidence to an area southeast of the Dead Sea. More significantly, the discovery of ancient crushed skeletons in the area, and also of fault lines in nearby rock faces, suggests that during the early Bronze Age an earthquake occurred measuring at least 6 on the Richter scale. Further geological evidence indicates that the earthquake could have caused major landslides from a process called 'liquefaction', whereby an earthquake forces water through the ground and destabilizes the soil. On sloping land, this would produce a landslide powerful enough to wipe out the Bronze Age buildings.

DESTRUCTION FROM THE SKY

So what of the reference to the rain of sulphur? This can be explained by the presence of naturally occurring sulphurous bitumen deposits in the Dead Sea. These deposits could have been thrown into the air when the earthquake struck, raining down over the habitations and even igniting if in contact with open flame. Chapter 19:28 of Genesis recounts that Abraham looked towards Sodom and Gomorrah, and 'saw dense smoke rising from the land, like smoke from a furnace', suggestive of a great land disturbance. While there remains much we cannot be sure of, we can no longer explain the destruction of Sodom and Gomorrah as simply biblical myth. ■

Lot, the nephew of Abraham, escaped from Sodom with his wife and two daughters. Although his wife paid the ultimate penalty for ignoring the advice of angels, the rest of the family survived by not looking back.

SALT IN THE INDUS VALLEY

SALT IS NOT A SUBSTANCE THAT WE NORMALLY ASSOCIATE WITH DISASTERS. YET SALT HAS IN THE PAST PRECIPITATED THE DOWNFALL OF ENTIRE CIVILIZATIONS, SUCH AS OCCURRED IN THE SECOND MILLENNIUM BC IN THE INDUS VALLEY, IN WHAT IS NOW INDIA AND PAKISTAN.

Between 3000 and 1500 BC, the Indus Valley harboured some of the most advanced and spectacular civilizations of the world.

COLLAPSING CIVILIZATION

From archaeological evidence unearthed in the 1920s, it is known that the valley had two major centres of habitation, Mohenjo-Daro and Harappa (the Indus Valley civilizations are also known as 'Harappan civilizations'). These cities had fully fledged urban administrations, and featured sophisticated housing (built on a grid pattern) and drainage systems, residential and commercial zones of habitation, standardized systems of weights and measures, and the organized production of valuable artefacts.

By 1500 BC, this entire civilization had collapsed. Although scientists and historians still debate the causes of its disappearance, most now point to soil salinity as a primary cause. All urban systems ➡➡

KEY FACTS

c.2000 BC – the Indus Valley contains some of the most sophisticated civilizations known in the world, comparable with those of Egypt and China.

Use of the Indus River to irrigate the fields results in destructive levels of salinity in the soil, and crop failure.

By 1500 BC, the Indus Valley civilizations have suffered a major collapse as harvests fail, a collapse from which they never recover.

The Indus Valley, once the centre of one of the world's most advanced civilizations, is littered with the remains of its former cultures, which collapsed around 1500 BC due to the salinization of agricultural land.

Above: Harappan culture was very sophisticated in terms of its urban developments. Unfortunately, the populations of the towns and cities remained acutely dependent upon the fertility and crop yields of the surrounding agricultural land.

require a surplus of agricultural produce to exist – the surplus allows people to engage in activities other than working the land. Harappan culture was no exception, with barley and wheat being the main crops (the region provides the first historical record of a systematically ploughed field).

CROP FAILURE

The presence of high levels of salt in agricultural land makes growing crops all but impossible, the salt restricting the amount of water the plant can absorb and adversely altering the chemical environment to make it detrimental to the plants. (The impact of 'salted land' is such that when the Romans sacked Carthage in 146 BC, they did not simply kill thousands of inhabitants and destroy the buildings, they also spread salt over Carthage's farmland to render it barren.) It appears that as the populations of the Indus Valley expanded, larger crop yields were required and additional irrigation. The farmers of the time brought water in from the Indus River, which diverted salts and lye from the mountain waters into the fields and slowly sterilized the land. Steadily, the creeping salinity strangled the entire Indus Valley, and by 1500 BC it was left to ruin as the people abandoned crops and houses. Even today salinity is a major problem within the area. ■

A view of the ruins in the Indus Valley, giving an impression of the scale of the lost civilization.

THERA VOLCANO

NOT ALL DISASTERS ARE DEFINED SOLELY BY A LOSS OF HUMAN LIFE. SOME REPRESENT GREAT CULTURAL LOSS OR THE DISPLACEMENT OF PEOPLES, AND AN ANCIENT EXAMPLE OF THIS COMES FROM THE AEGEAN ISLAND OF THERA, ABOUT 100KM (60 MILES) NORTH OF CRETE.

By the 17th century BC, Thera was an important part of the Greek world, primarily because of its major port, located around what is today Akrotiri (the modern name given to the ancient site).

IMPENDING DISASTER

Akrotiri ranked among the most highly developed habitations of its period. Its densely packed, multistorey housing was well served by paved streets, an effective underground sewerage system and rainwater channels. Modern archaeological investigations have revealed that the houses themselves had sophisticated interior decoration, which featured elaborate, naturalistic frescoes, typically portraying religious processions or maritime themes. However, Akrotiri was also in an area of high seismic activity and was overshadowed by a nearby active volcano.

Unlike many ancient (and modern) civilizations, Akrotiri shows clear signs of anti-earthquake building construction – masonry walls were buttressed with additional horizontal and vertical timber ➤➤

KEY FACTS

17th century BC – Akrotiri, on the Aegean island of Thera, develops into a major port.

c.1628 BC – The residents of Akrotiri abandon the town following increased volcanic and seismic activity.

Akrotiri is entirely destroyed by a huge volcanic eruption, which buries the urban area in tons of volcanic deposits.

The modern island of Thera is now a major tourist destination. Mainland Greece remains a seismically sensitive region, suffering more earth tremors than any other country in Europe.

➤➤

supports. However, in 1628 BC severe tremors flexed the town, terrifying the inhabitants enough for them to make a mass exodus from their homes. They returned shortly afterwards to attempt reconstruction, but evidence suggests that they rapidly abandoned their efforts as the Thera volcano dominating the island began to erupt.

ASH CLOUD

No preserved human remains or valuable artefacts have been found at Akrotiri, suggesting that the evacuation was successful, but when the volcano finally erupted it ensured that no one would ever inhabit Akrotiri again. The eruption ejected an estimated 31 cubic kilometres (7.5 cubic miles) of magma into the air and generated a 79 cubic kilometre (19 cubic mile) pyroclastic event. Along with the tons of ash deposited during the early stages of the eruption, this sealed Akrotiri in a volcanic grave, and preserved the town well for future archaeologists. The Thera volcano collapsed, creating a massive caldera (crater), into which the sea rushed in a huge tidal wave. Some historians have accredited the Thera explosion with the downfall of the entire Minoan civilization (see next entry). ■

Above: Minoan civilization was at its height in the second millennium BC, and its former palace cultures have yielded rich stores of artefacts.

This aerial view of Thera clearly shows the caldera between the two landmasses. Destruction of such large landmasses usually generates terrible tsunami, and today volcanic activity on the Canary Islands poses a similar threat.

CRETAN TSUNAMI

A NATURAL DISASTER IN ONE LOCATION CAN PRECIPITATE A SUBSEQUENT, AND WORSE, DISASTER AT ANOTHER LOCATION, AND THE VOLCANIC ERUPTION ON THERA DESCRIBED IN THE PREVIOUS ENTRY IS A GOOD CASE IN POINT.

The volcano that erupted *c.*1650 BC was located in the northern half of the island.

SHIFTING LANDMASS

Such was the sheer violence of the eruption that it literally blew the volcano and much of the island to pieces, removing about 82 square kilometres (32 square miles) of the island's landmass. The result was the formation of a caldera, essentially a bowl-shaped depression caused by the volcano collapsing in on itself. The surrounding Aegean Sea rushed to fill this huge depression, and the massive displacement of water combined with huge aquatic detonations as the seawater came into contact with the volcano's underlying magma. Radiating out from Thera came tsunami measuring up to 150m (492ft) high and moving at around 160km/h (100mph). ➻

KEY FACTS

c.1650 – Huge volcanic eruption on the Aegean island of Thera generates a tsunami up to 150m (492ft) high.

The tsunami strikes the northern coastline of Crete, demolishing fishing fleets, habitations and some of the island's finest palaces.

Crete subsequently enters a period of cultural instability and decline.

Prior to the earthquake of 1650 BC, Crete was one of the most powerful of the Greek islands. The tsunami generated from the Theran explosion rose to an estimated 150m (492ft) in height prior to its impact on the Cretan coastline.

Some 110km (70 miles) away from the Thera explosion was the northern coastline of Crete. Minoan Crete was at this time reaching the zenith of its cultural and political power, with great palace civilizations at locations such as Knossos and Mallia, both on the northern coast. When the wave struck Crete – the wall of water taking only minutes to cross the Aegean – massive damage was done to the Cretan coastal infrastructure, wrecking the fleet of ships anchored off shore, wiping out domestic habitations and causing likely destruction to the palaces and surrounding buildings.

DECLINING CIVILIZATION

Archaeological finds also show that east Crete was choked by the vast clouds of pumice and ash drifting down from Thera, and this in turn led to great problems with agricultural pollution. Because the Theran eruption lies close to the beginnings of recorded history, there is no way of assessing casualty figures. However, what is known is that the decline of Minoan Crete's palace period is dated from around the time of the eruption, so it is likely that the volcano not only destroyed much of Thera, but also brought about the disruption and decline of one of the most advanced civilizations of the time. ■

Above: A depiction of the advanced coastal cultures typical of Greece during the second millennium BC. Coastlines have traditionally attracted the bulk of human urban development, which is one reason why tsunami cause such a huge loss of life.

Ash clouds from a volcano have an enormous environmental impact. Not only do the desposits choke plant growth and affect the availability of animal food, but the airborne clouds blot out the sun and cause a drop in temperatures as well.

PLAGUE OF ATHENS

THE GREAT PLAGUE THAT OVERWHELMED ATHENS IN 429 BC CAME AT A TIME WHEN THE CITY WAS SPREADING ITS IMPERIAL POWER THROUGHOUT GREECE, AND HAD COME INTO CONFLICT WITH SPARTA AND ITS PELOPONNESIAN ALLIES.

Our main descriptive source for the plague's effect is Thucydides (*c*.460–400 BC), the ancient historian and early anthropologist who devotes a lengthy passage to the epidemic in his *History of the Peloponnesian War.*

PLAGUE STRIKES
The plague could not have come at a worse time for the Athenians, as the forces of the Peloponnesian alliance had just invaded Attica and were ransacking the region. Thucydides points to isolated cases of plague in Athens prior to the epidemic, but nothing on the scale of the one that struck the city in 429 BC. The first cases emerged around Piraeus, the harbour at Athens (supporting some suggestions that the plague was imported into Greece from North Africa or Persia), then ran through the general population like wildfire. Although recovery did occur, Thucydides describes ➤➤

KEY FACTS

- **429 BC** – Plague takes hold of Athens during the Peloponnesian War, killing around one third of the city's population.
- **The spread** of the disease is aided by overcrowding of the city by war refugees and soldiers.
- **Plague would** strike again in Athens in 427 BC.

During the plague, corpses piled up at such a rate that they were burned without ceremony on the outskirts of the city.

➤➤

a horrific list of symptoms, beginning with oral bleeding and terminating in chronic systemic failure and usually death.

SOCIAL COLLAPSE

The virility of the disease is conveyed by Thucydides: 'Those with naturally strong constitutions were no better able than the weak to resist the disease, which carried away all alike, even those who were treated and dieted with the greatest care.' The spread of the disease was assisted by an ingress of people, relocating because of the war from rural Attica into Athens. As housing was already limited, the new inhabitants were located in overcrowded, temporary shelters, which enabled the disease to concentrate itself. Huge piles of bodies soon littered the streets, and normal ritualistic funerary procedures were abandoned for mass burials and huge cremations. Thucydides also paints a picture of a spreading lawlessness in the city – 'As for offences against human law, no one expected to live long enough to be brought to trial and punished.' It has been estimated that around one-third of the population of Athens died during the plague; even the Greek leader Pericles was himself killed by the illness. A retro-diagnosis of the illness is difficult, primarily because diseases change in nature over time, but the symptoms described by Thucydides make typhus a likely candidate. ∎

Pericles was the highest-profile victim of the Athenian plague, which cost tens of thousands of lives.

IMPERIAL DISASTERS
AD 1 – 1000

The growth of city cultures provided one of the key ingredients for a major disaster – large concentrations of people confined in relatively small areas of land. The catastrophic volcanic eruption of Vesuvius in AD 79 would have been a relatively minor affair had it occurred in a sparsely populated agricultural area. Instead, the volcano's pyroclastic flows struck Herculaneum, Pompeii and Stabiae, killing thousands of people instantly. Cities also brought the danger of fire, as open flames served for light, heat and cooking, and buildings were usually constructed of highly flammable natural materials.

Left: Milan in 539 saw 300,000 people killed in one of the worst massacres in history.

GREAT FIRE OF ROME

THE GREAT FIRE OF ROME, WHICH OCCURRED IN AD 64, IS BOTH A MAJOR DISASTER AND AN HISTORICAL MYSTERY.

It was on the night of 19 July that fire broke out among the shopping stalls of the Circus Maximus, Rome's huge central sports stadium. Used mainly for chariot and horse racing, it had a capacity for 250,000 people. The fire spread quickly – high summer in Rome made the city into a tinderbox of dry, densely packed wooden housing, and regular fires were common. This time, however, the fire took on a scale never previously seen. It spread throughout the city and the principal narrator of the events, Tacitus, recounts that 'terrified, screaming women, the helpless old and young, people seeking their own safety, people unselfishly helping invalids … all heightened the confusion'.

THE CONFLAGRATION

The fire burned for nine days in total, killing hundreds and wiping out 10 of Rome's 14 districts. Most controversial was Emperor Nero's response to the fire. Many people, including Tacitus, hinted that Nero was complicit in the fire, as he had recently been ➤➤

KEY FACTS

- **19 July 64** – Fire breaks out in the Circus Maximus, Rome.
- **28 July** – The fire finally burns itself out, but not before having destroyed two-thirds of the city of Rome.
- **Rumours circulate** that the Emperor Nero was behind the blaze. Nero turns on the Christians as scapegoats.

In AD 64, Rome was at the height of its imperial power. The reforms of the Emperor Augustus had made the city into the most modern urban centre in the world, featuring advanced water and drainage systems, a professional administration and architectural masterpieces. Two-thirds of this city would be lost in the fire.

Above: The Christians were a convenient scapegoat for Nero following the great fire in Rome. Persecution dogged the Christian community under Roman rule for three centuries, until Christianity was adopted as a state religion under the rule of Constantine in AD 313.

thwarted by the Senate in his plans to develop a large series of palaces throughout Rome. Certainly, in the aftermath of the fire, Nero began building the Domus Aurea (Gold House), a huge landscaped area of villas and pavilions constructed directly on the areas incinerated by the blaze. Tacitus also claimed that armed gangs (possibly in the pay of the government) prevented people from fighting the fires, and actively fed the blaze with flaming torches.

PLACING BLAME

Nero was away from Rome when the fire broke out, safely in his palace at Antium, but in his defence it must be said that he returned quickly to Rome and organized teams of firefighters. Furthermore, he provided thousands of homeless people with shelter and also suffered personal loss – one of his newest properties, the Domus Transitoria, was burnt to the ground. Whatever the state of affairs, Nero soon found a scapegoat for the great fire in the form of the emergent Christian sect. Thousands of Christians were channelled into the gladiatorial arenas, where they were killed by wild animals or human hands for the entertainment of the Romans. In Nero's eyes, someone had to pay for the destruction of two-thirds of the imperial city. ■

Some of Rome's most famous landmarks were destroyed in the fire of AD 64, although it spread mainly through residential areas.

POMPEII

IN AD 79, THE CITIZENS OF POMPEII HAD LIVED IN THE SHADOW OF MOUNT VESUVIUS FOR HUNDREDS OF YEARS.

The volcano was actually a blessing – the fertile volcanic soil gave the area excellent agricultural growth. However, on 24 August the volcano finally turned on Pompeii's citizens.

WARNING SIGNS

The eruption had been preceded by several days of geological phenomena. There were minor earth tremors, as well as significant changes in the flow speed and levels of nearby watercourses. Animals were also behaving strangely, with dogs, cats and livestock seeming agitated. Finally, in the early afternoon of the 24th, Vesuvius erupted with a massive explosion. The first stage of the eruption saw a gargantuan cloud of pumice, rocks and ash climb as high as 20km (12 miles) into the atmosphere, then begin to settle back onto the ground. These deposits fell in a thick, scalding-hot blanket on Pompeii's streets, 10km (6 miles) away from Vesuvius, at a rate of 15cm (6in) per hour. The citizens of another town, Herculaneum, were actually nearer the eruption, but escaped the ash by being downwind. Although a number of people were killed by falling rocks and asphyxiation in Pompeii, the greatest danger was ➥

KEY FACTS

24 August 79, 1.30 p.m. – Mount Vesuvius erupts, creating a vast cloud of tephra (volcanic emissions), which falls on Pompeii for around eight hours.

Huge ash deposits on Pompeii crush many buildings.

11.30 p.m. – A succession of pyroclastic flows begins from the volcano and wipes out Herculaneum, Stabiae and Pompeii.

Pompeii's ruins are now a major tourist attraction. The massive output of volcanic emissions submerged much of the city in ash deposits, and these served to preserve the ruins for future generations.

➤➤

the build-up of ash crushing homes with its weight. For eight hours, the ash kept falling, stacking up to a height of 2–4m (8–10ft). Thousands of the city's people evacuated and headed out into the countryside, leaving only an unfortunate 10 per cent of the population behind.

SCORCHED EARTH

Night came, the darkness showing up a spectacular fireworks display from Vesuvius. Shortly before midnight, the nature of the eruption tragically changed. The huge column of superheated debris rising from the volcano began to collapse, and turned into a pyroclastic flow of molten pumice and rock, which rolled down the volcano side at hundreds of miles an hour and temperatures of 398°C (750°F). Herculaneum was engulfed and razed, along with all inhabitants, in a matter of seconds. Further flows fell short of Pompeii, until a final blast at 6.30 a.m. wiped the city from the face of the earth, the 2000 citizens being scalded and asphyxiated to death in seconds. Both Herculaneum, Pompeii and nearby Stabiae were buried under tons of concrete-hard ash, in places up to 20m (65ft) deep. Vesuvius has erupted nearly 500 times since AD 79, and today threatens the huge Italian city of Naples, with its population of more than one million. ■

The open countryside was one of the few places of safety during the eruption of Mount Vesuvius in AD 79, *although a distance of just several miles from the volcano was enough to ensure protection from the pyroclastic flows.*

ROMAN PLAGUE

AT THE END OF THE SECOND MILLENNIUM AD, ROME HAD ATTAINED ITS POSITION OF IMPERIAL GREATNESS.

Around AD 100, Rome's empire stretched from North Africa to Britain, and from Rome to as far east as Syria. This awesome level of expansion placed Rome in a state of almost constant war, but in AD 180 Rome was faced by an enemy that was almost impossible to fight and which caused far more deaths than any battlefield action – plague.

ORIGINS OF THE PLAGUE

What the plague actually was is difficult to ascertain. It could have been bubonic plague, which originated in central Asia and has been a regular visitor to western Europe for the past 2500 years. Alternatively, smallpox could have been the affliction. Whatever the type of illness, it is certain that Rome was a city acutely vulnerable to any sort of serious infectious disease. Its population in the second century AD was around one million, far in excess of any other major city in the world at that time. Despite the city planning reforms of Augustus (emperor from 27 BC to AD 14), ➤➤

KEY FACTS

AD 180 – Rome struck by plague, the disease most likely being imported into the city from Parthia.

One in 10 Romans dies between 180 and 189.

Plague results in a huge depletion of manpower available for military service.

The plague was interpreted by many Romans as being the visitation of divine wrath upon the population.

Above: Marcus Aurelius was one of Rome's great emperors, renowned for his wisdom. His collections of Meditations *reflect frequently on the fragility and fleeting nature of existence and wealth, a message that the plague would have strongly reinforced.*

sanitation was poor. Furthermore, its empire meant that Rome had a large and regular ingress of foreign peoples, who brought with them diseases for which their was no immunity among the indigenous Romans. The plague struck around 180, and some believe it was brought into Rome by the Legions of Marcus Aurelius returning to Rome from fighting in Parthia.

POTENT KILLER

The plague ripped through Roman society, and at its height was killing around 2000 people every day. One-tenth of Rome died over the next nine years, and certain locales lost one-third of their population. Nor was the disease confined just to Rome, but spread throughout the rest of Italy and out to Asia Minor, Greece and Egypt. Ultimately, the plague was more than a periodic health disaster for the Romans; it was a disaster for the empire. Thousands of army troops died, and this (along with other social causes) led to an increased reliance on mercenaries, who did not have the same emotional commitment to the defence of Rome as native troops. The workforce was also depleted, leading to economic difficulties. The plague and subsequent periods of disease were significant factors in the gradual collapse of the Roman empire, which was completed by the fifth century. ∎

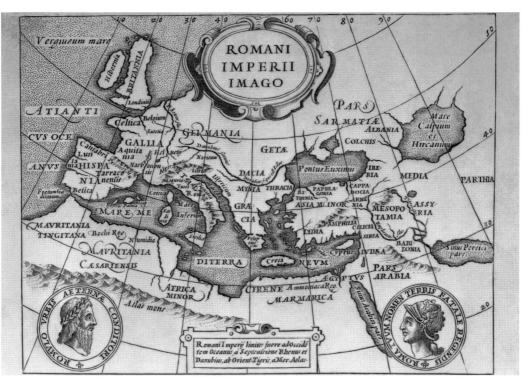

The Roman empire incorporated much of the known world at the time, and its trade routes facilitated the spread of disease.

ANTIOCH EARTHQUAKE

BY THE SIXTH CENTURY AD, ANTIOCH WAS A CITY OF POWER AND SPLENDOUR. BUT IT WAS LOCATED IN ONE OF THE WORLD'S MOST SEISMICALLY VOLATILE REGIONS.

Now located in southern Turkey, and called Antakya, it had been absorbed into the Roman Empire in 64 BC, becoming the capital of Rome's Syrian province and the third-largest city in the empire, a centre of fine architecture and a lively intellectual culture.

The city was no stranger to earthquakes. In 115 AD, the Emperor Trajan was in the city with his army when a tremor shook the urban foundations, altered the course of its waterways and caused hundreds of deaths. Earthquakes came again in 341 and in 458, when half the city was wiped out, the impact of the quake compounded by a large fire that followed in its wake. However, the most destructive seismic events occurred in 526.

DISASTER RELIEF

The year before, Antioch had been severely damaged by a city-wide fire, and was just recovering from this when an earthquake of enormous magnitude hit. This time almost all of the city was ➤➤

KEY FACTS

115, 341 and 458 AD – Antioch suffers major earthquakes, which kill thousands of its inhabitants.

526 – The city is almost entirely destroyed by an earthquake that kills a quarter of a million people.

Nearly 75,000 people will die in subsequent earthquakes between 526 and 588.

Antioch was cursed by a series of major earthquakes, each one destroying huge portions of the city and costing hundreds of thousands of lives. Today, very little remains of the ancient city besides isolated artefacts and foundations.

Above: Antioch was frequently fought over during the wars between the Christian West and Muslim East, battles which hampered earthquake recovery.

wiped out, with the death toll rising to 250,000. The number of fatalities was worsened by Christian gatherings, which concentrated people within buildings that collapsed.

RECONSTRUCTION

The empire was shocked by the devastation, and the loss of such great buildings as the octagonal cathedral built by Constantinus II. The emperor in Constantinople, Justin I, mounted what is an early example of a relief operation. It is reported that he spent 900kg (2000lb) of gold for reconstruction. Yet Antioch's seismic curse was not finished.

In 528, the city was once again hit, with 5000 killed, and in 588 some 60,000 people died during another earthquake. (At one point, the city was renamed Theopolis – City of God – in the hope of obtaining divine favour.) Severe earthquakes continue in the region to this day. ∎

Antioch's seismic troubles extended well beyond the medieval period and into the nineteenth century, with the city being badly damaged by an earthquake in 1872.

PLAGUE OF JUSTINIAN

THE PLAGUE HAS BEEN A DEVASTATING VISITOR TO WORLD HISTORY SINCE THE EARLIEST TIMES.

Some scientists believe that a disease described in the Bible, 1 Samuel, can be attributed as being bubonic plague, this giving the disease a historical start date of around 1320 BC. However, more historically verifiable accounts of plague date from the first century AD, from Libya, Egypt and Syria, with observers describing the buboes that would become so terribly well known during the medieval period. The first recorded plague pandemic, however, can be accurately determined as starting in the city of Constantinople in around 542.

IMPERIAL DISASTER

By 540, Constantinople was the centre of the powerful Byzantine empire, which spread from North Africa through the Middle East, swallowing the Balkans. It was one of the most prestigious cities on earth, its art and architecture regarded as the finest in the world, and its bureaucratic administration overseen by the emperor Justinian, who had taken the throne in 527. However, the ➤➤

KEY FACTS

- **542** – plague strikes Constantinople, having moved up from Egypt via trade routes.
- **Around 40–50 per cent** of the population die, with the death rate peaking at 10,000 people per day.
- **The plague** radiates outwards across Europe and Asia, killing 100 million people.

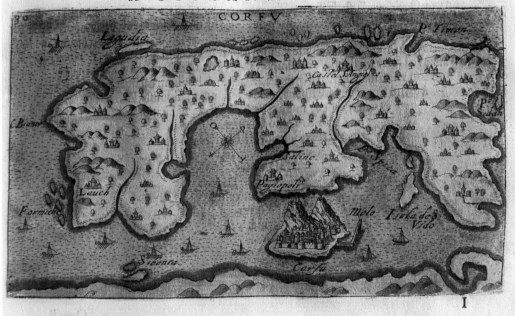

Constantinople was the most important city in the world during the sixth century AD. Byzantium was chosen as the new capital of the Roman Empire by Constantine in 326 AD.

incorporation of Egypt into its empire was almost to prove the city's undoing. By 542, the plague was already present in Egypt, and soon travelled by overland and maritime trade routes to Constantinople itself.

DECIMATED POPULATION

The effect upon the city could not have been more devastating. According to the writings of Procopius of Caesarea, the illness was killing around 10,000 people every day at its peak, and there are estimates that around 50 per cent of the entire city died. Such was the problem of corpse disposal that towers were used as mass burial chambers, the roofs being removed and quick lime then poured in to hasten decomposition. An alternative was to fill ships with bodies, then push the ships out to sea, setting them on fire.

The armies of the Byzantine empire were decimated by the illness, leading to a prolonged period of social unrest and war. Nor did the plague stop in Constantinople. The disease spread as far west as Britain and as far east as China, and by 1610 it had killed an estimated 100 million people. Constantinople was to be visited again by the plague in 732, again losing around 40 per cent of its people. ■

Above: The plague would challenge Byzantium's Christian faith. The contemporary writer Procopius stated: 'this calamity it is quite impossible either to express in words or to conceive in thought any explanation, except indeed to refer it to God.'

Byzantium was a place of great artistic treasure and social wealth. However, its extensive trade networks, which stretched throughout eastern Europe and the Balkans, made the city vulnerable to the importation of diseases.

THE MASSACRE OF MILAN

THE FIFTH AND SIXTH CENTURIES WERE A DIFFICULT PERIOD FOR THE CIVILIANS OF ITALY.

Europe during this time was in a state of bloody flux as the Roman Empire disintegrated. Goths, Franks, Byzantines and the Italians themselves all struggled for possession of the Italian mainland, and in 493 the Ostrogothic leader Theodoric had established control over all Italian territory.

GOTHIC ASSAULT

Despite the 'barbarian' reputation, the rule of Theodoric was initially relatively stable; however, during the early sixth century religious, ethnic and imperial tensions pulled the country once again into war. In 535, after Theodoric's death, the Byzantine general Belisarius was sent by the eastern emperor Justinian to invade and occupy Sicily before crossing to the mainland and advancing to take Milan by 538.

The Gothic king in Italy, Witigis, was incensed by what he saw as the treachery of the Milanese. In 539, he dispatched a large army, bolstered by 10,000 Burgundians to retake the ➤➤

KEY FACTS

535 – the Byzantine general Belisarius begins a campaign to take over Italy from Ostrogothic rule.

538 – the Byzantine forces occupy Milan, but the city is placed under siege by the Goths in 539.

March 539 – Milan surrenders, and the Goths murder around 300,000 of the population.

The Goths took no pity on the population of Milan, with almost all of the city's citizens being murdered or enslaved.

Above: Theodoric the Great was regarded as a judicious and circumspect ruler. He was the founder of the Ostrogoth kingdom in Italy.

city. A shadow was now falling over Milan. The city soon found itself besieged, with the walls held by only 300 soldiers and its civilian population.

PITILESS WARRIORS

Milan's commander Mundilas sent out messages to Belisarius, pleading for assistance. Imperial politics delayed the help, however, and the city's people began to starve. Soon the inhabitants were reduced to eating dogs, cats and mice, and under such conditions the residents of Milan became ever more susceptible to the Gothic requests for their surrender, and the promises of clemency towards the population. Mundilas initially resisted, but eventually even his soldiers pleaded with him to surrender, which they did towards the end of March.

All the promises of humane treatment from the Goths and Franks would count for nothing in the end. In what was one of the worst massacres in history, 300,000 people (according to the contemporary historian Procopius) were put to the sword – every male in the city and thousands of women and children. The surviving women were shipped off for a life of abject slavery in the service of the Goths. Milan had paid the ultimate price for succumbing to the imperial Byzantines. ∎

The Goths were a warrior people who originated in southern Scandinavia during the sixth century AD.

CORINTH EARTHQUAKE

THE ANCIENT CITY OF CORINTH SAT IN THE PELOPONNESE, ROUGHLY 80KM (50 MILES) WEST OF ATHENS.

It developed as a commercially oriented city state from around the eighth century BC, and the city would grow to be a dominant force on the maritime trade routes between the Aegean and Ionian seas. Only in the sixth century BC was its pre-eminence in the region eclipsed by the rising star of Athens. For the next 500 years, Corinth was a troubled player in the region's perennial power struggles, and in 44 BC it became a Roman colony. Under the Romans, Corinth physically and politically expanded, and although the Roman Empire drew to a close around the fifth century AD, the city remained of considerable stature.

CITY DESTROYED

Unfortunately for the Corinthians, however, the city also sat on top of the one of the most seismically active regions in all Europe. Scientists currently studying the Gulf of Corinth's tectonic activity have claimed that the region is likely to have the fastest continental rift on the planet, the plates opening at a rate of up to 1.5cm ➤➤

KEY FACTS

850s – the ancient city of Corinth in the Peloponnese is struck by a succession of damaging earthquakes.

856 – the city is almost entirely destroyed by a huge earthquake, probably of 8 or 9 magnitude, which kills 45,000 people.

The region is affected by seismic activity to this day.

An impressive view of the ruins of ancient Corinth, giving an impression of the geological activity of the region as well as the urban splendour that once defined the city.

➥

Above: Corinth's ruins include the formerly spectacular Temple of Apollo and the Agora (market place), which was once the site of much of the city's trade. Earthquakes would bring the cultural life of the city to near shut-down on several occasions.

(0.59in) per year. In AD 856, such powerful seismic forces were about to unleash themselves upon the city.

CENTURY OF DISASTER

The ninth century AD was a generally bleak time for Corinth in terms of its relationship with seismic activity. During the early 850s, the city suffered from a series of major tremors, which killed hundreds and had a profound impact on the city's social and economic welfare. These troubles culminated in an enormous earthquake in 856, which almost entirely demolished the city. The earthquake still ranks as one of the worst seismic disasters in history, with an estimated 45,000 people being killed. The magnitude of the earthquake is not recorded, but it is likely to have been around 9 or 10 on the Mercalli scale. Combined with social and political factors, the earthquakes were a major reason for the final withering away of ancient Corinth, and in 1858 another massive earthquake finally quashed the viability of the city. Modern Corinth is located 5km (3 miles) northeast of the ancient city, but has itself not escaped the seismic volatility of the region. It was severely damaged by earthquakes in 1928 and 1981, and seismologists are working hard to develop effective predictors of the next earthquake. ■

During Corinth's many earthquakes, the widespread presence of monumental masonry and multistorey buildings contributed to the massive death toll, as people were killed by falling stonework.

MEDIEVAL DISASTERS
1000 – 1500

The medieval world was struck by disaster on a global scale in the form of the Black Death. This horrific killer, which took the lives of one in three Europeans, showed how terribly vulnerable the human race was to a disease that was easily transmitted and against which there was no immunity. Lethal disease is a constant visitor to the medieval period, and the beginnings of transoceanic colonization in the fifteenth century ensured that European diseases were exported globally, often with devastating effects upon the indigenous populations. A drop in global temperatures, beginning what is known as the Little Ice Age, also added to a time of great social trauma.

Left: Scenes from the horrific black death which killed up to 33 per cent of the entire population of Europe.

JERUSALEM

THE SIEGE AND FALL OF JERUSALEM IN 1099 WAS A MILITARY DISASTER (FOR THE DEFENDERS), AND TURNED INTO A GREAT HUMAN TRAGEDY.

Jerusalem had fallen under Muslim rule after a 48-day siege in 1098, and so became a prime objective of the Christian knights and infantry of the First Crusade (1095–1100), who had advanced from the Balkans into the Holy Land by 1097.

FALL AND SLAUGHTER

Knowing that the Crusaders would be on their way, the Muslim garrison of Jerusalem, led by the capable commander Iftikhar al-Dawla, repaired damage to the outer walls, and built up the earthwork and ditch defences ringing the city. Al-Dawla also prepared for a siege, stockpiling food and water, cutting down local trees to deny the Crusaders use of timber, and poisoning wells outside the city to reduce the enemy's water supply. He also expelled many of the city's Christians.

Initially, al-Dawla's measures seemed to pay off. The Crusaders reached Jerusalem on 7 June 1099 and attacked it on 13 June, with no success. Hence they began a siege action. Around 1500 knights and 5000 infantry ringed Jerusalem, but their numbers were quickly reduced by lack of water and food, ➧

> **KEY FACTS**
>
> **1098** – Jerusalem is occupied by Muslim forces after a 48-day siege.
> **13 June 1099** – Christian forces of the First Crusade put Jerusalem under siege.
> **15 July** – Jerusalem falls to the Crusaders, who massacre the entire population of the city, around 90,000 people.

The first Crusade was conducted from 1095 to 1101, and the last of eight such expeditions was in 1270.

Above: A Crusader cavalryman. Cavalry was the principal combat arm for most armies during the medieval period, the mounted soldiers being used to break open the enemy lines, conduct ambushes and reconnaissance, and perform flanking and encirclement manoeuvres.

as well as spreading disease. However, a fleet of Christian ships arrived at Jaffa on 17 June, and the ships' timbers were used to make three siege towers, completed during the first week of July. On 13 July, the Crusaders began to advance the towers towards the walls of Jerusalem. Initial efforts failed, but one tower managed to site itself next to the northeastern gate on 15 July, and the Crusaders began flooding into the city.

CHRISTIAN MASSACRE

What happened next is one of the most appalling episodes in Christian history. The Crusaders systematically killed almost every man, woman and child in the city. Brutalized by long months of war and hardship, the soldiers massacred almost every one they came upon, including Christians, and slaughtered a vast crowd of refugees in the al-Aqsa mosque. One contemporary account observed that 'the slaughter was so great that our men waded in blood up to their ankles'. Ironically, only al-Dawla and his bodyguard survived, after they surrendered when surrounded by enemy soldiers. It has been estimated that some 90,000 people were put to the sword in Jerusalem. In a reflection of the times, in Christian Europe, bells were rung to celebrate the 'victory'. ∎

Christian knights pray before Jerusalem. By the time the Crusaders took Jerusalem in 1099, they had already lost thousands of men to battle and disease, and were running low on the spirit of mercy.

THE LITTLE ICE AGE

THE 'LITTLE ICE AGE' (LIA) – AS THE PHENOMENON IS NOW
KNOWN BY CLIMATOLOGISTS – WAS NOT AN IMMEDIATE DISASTER
SUCH AS AN EARTHQUAKE OR VOLCANO, BUT A PROLONGED
CLIMATE EVENT THAT PRODUCED DISASTROUS EFFECTS OVER
A LONG PERIOD.

Between the thirteenth century and the nineteenth century,
the northern hemisphere was to experience a steady plunge in
average temperatures, the height of the event being between
about 1550 and 1850.

SHORTER HARVESTS

The causes of the LIA are much debated and remain controversial,
but the principal reasons put forward are a general decrease in
solar activity and an increase in global volcanic activity, the
volcanic emissions clouding the atmosphere and so reducing the
sunlight penetrating through to ground. Whatever the causes, the
temperatures fell to record levels during the increasingly long
winters – the winters became so icy that on occasions the
inhabitants of New York could walk from Manhattan to Staten ➤➤

KEY FACTS

13th–19th centuries – the
Northern Hemisphere
experiences a dramatic
cooling, bringing extreme
arctic winter conditions and
cool, wet summers.
The 'Little Ice Age' has
a devastating effect on
agriculture, resulting in
widespread, recurrent
famines, which kill millions.
Global temperatures begin to
rise again around 1850.

Although the Little Ice Age brought some social benefits, such as ice skating, it was a catastrophe for crop production.

➡ Island across New York harbour, and the population of London could also walk across the river Thames. Yet there were numerous detrimental social effects which ultimately cost the lives of millions.

GLOBAL EFFECTS

In agriculture, the available growing season was shortened by up to two months, reducing not only the amount of crops available, but also the amount of seed left at the end of the year for planting, and encouraging the growth of fungus on crops during the cool, wet summers. Livestock also died through cold and lack of feed. Famine resulted – 1.5 million people died in Europe in 1315, and France's crop failure of 1693 produced several million deaths, these being just two examples of the LIA death toll. In far northern climates, increases in glaciation and snowfall wiped out entire towns and, in some cases, civilizations – the population of Iceland fell by 50 per cent and the Vikings of Greenland died out entirely. The freezing temperatures weakened people's immunity, therefore aiding the spread of epidemics such as the plague. The LIA also precipitated great social unrest, and there was an intensification of witch-hunting as people looked for theological scapegoats. Only around 1850 did the world finally start warming, a pattern that is of so much concern today. ■

The Little Ice Age occurred during a time of history when the world population was in steep growth, particularly in Europe. This expansion meant the effects of crop failure were greatly exacerbated, with continent-wide famines killing millions.

SEA OF JAPAN

SOME DISASTERS ARE CATASTROPHIC FOR THOSE INVOLVED, BUT PROVE TO BE A BLESSING FOR OTHERS. A CLASSIC EXAMPLE OF THIS PARADOX OCCURRED IN 1274 AD WITH THE DESTRUCTION OF THE FLEET OF KUBLAI KHAN.

During the thirteenth century, the Mongols were ascendant in east Asia. The Mongolian leader Kublai Khan, grandson of the great warrior Genghis Khan, became the ruler of all China after a series of brilliant conquests between 1250 and 1279, completing one of the largest territorial empires in history. Following the final conquest of the Sung dynasty of southern China, Khan inaugurated a period of fairly judicious central administration, but was also at the same time casting his eyes around for further conquests. His gaze fell on Japan.

DIVINE WIND

The Mongols were primarily a land-based cavalry army, but the growth of the empire during the thirteenth century necessitated the development of a navy. From the 1270s, a fleet of warships and transport vessels was gradually produced, and by 1280s was ➤➤

The Mongol attempts to invade Japan in the thirteenth century were both thwarted by nature rather than by enemy action. The loss of 100,000 men in 1281 meant that all further invasion plans were called off.

Above: Kublai Khan (1215–1294) was one of the Mongols' most successful rulers, bringing the Mongol people under a professional administration while also expanding the empire.

capable of oceanic military operations. Meanwhile, Japan had been raising Kublai Khan's ire by resisting the making of treaties with the Mongols. In 1274, Kublai attempted a invasion of Japan, deploying 900 ships and 33,000 troops. However, bad storms at sea demolished much of the fleet, and 13,000 soldiers drowned.

DIVINE WIND

Kublai was furious at his plans coming to nought, so in 1281 he decided to try again, although with much greater force. He assembled 4400 ships, transporting a total of 150,000 soldiers/sailors. Mongol units were able to put ashore on Kyushu and occupy the area up to Dazaifu, 15km (9 miles) south of Fukuoka city, despite the fact that the Japanese defences were better than in previous years. Then, just before the Mongols launched their final major attack, a colossal typhoon struck the region. Many Mongol soldiers were still at sea, so they steered their vessels away from the dangerous coastline. There the typhoon wiped out almost all of the Mongol ships, resulting in the deaths of up to 100,000 men. The typhoon destroyed the Mongol invasion plans, and preserved the Japanese from almost certain occupation. Not surprisngly, the Japanese referred to the storms as *kamikaze,* meaning 'divine wind'. ■

A depiction of the Mongol invasion fleet, wrecked by a massive tropical typhoon. While the storm sent the majority of the vessels to the bottom of the sea, Japanese warships later went out to pick off any survivors they could find. Such was the fortuitous nature of the typhoon that the Japanese ascribed the storm to divine origins.

BLACK DEATH

THE ORIGINS OF THE BLACK DEATH ARE DIFFICULT TO ASCERTAIN, BUT IT APPEARS TO HAVE STARTED IN CHINA IN THE EARLY 1330s AND SPREAD VIA TRADE ROUTES THROUGH TO ASIA, THEN WESTERN EUROPE, WHERE IT STRUCK IN 1348.

The disease came in three basic varieties, all with acute mortality rates. Bubonic plague, named after the swellings (buboes) that appeared on the victim's body, had a 30–75 per cent mortality rate and was spread by rat fleas; pneumonic plague, with a rate of 90–95 per cent, was an airborne disease transmitted in the same way as influenza; and septicaemic plague caused acute blood poisoning and had a mortality rate of 99–100 per cent.

APOCALYPSE

Whatever the type of disease, the plague turned medieval Europe into a charnel house. It is hard to overstate the social impact of the Black Death. Entire households and communities could go from healthy to dead in a matter of a few days, sometimes overnight. Whole cities lost around 50 per cent of their inhabitants, urban areas being the most vulnerable to the disease because of ➤➤

KEY FACTS

1330s – plague originates in China and spreads to western Europe by 1338.

1338–51 – One-third of the European population dies from the effects of the plague, a total of around 75 million people, which had a catastrophic effect on the social, religious and economic fabric of society.

A powerful engraving that conveys the sheer horror of the plague. Those responsible for the burial of the huge numbers of dead were often given separate accommodation in churchyards to prevent them mixing with the wider population.

Above: The rat flea was the principal source of the Black Death, but over the centuries the disease mutated into several other lethal forms, including an airborne pneumonic form that had a 90 per cent mortality rate.

overcrowding and poor sanitation. Households infected with the plague were quarantined – and, in Milan, the authorities walled up diseased families in their own homes, a measure that resulted in Milan having one of the best records of controlling the disease within a large urban population.

NIGHTMARE WORLD

Bodies littered the streets in vast quantities. The writer of the *Decameron*, Giovanni Boccaccio, recorded that 'Dead bodies filled every corner … Although the cemeteries were full, they [the local people] were forced to dig huge trenches, where they buried the bodies by hundreds.' The art of the period commonly shows the figure of death riding through an apocalyptic landscape on a skeletal horse, and social order teetered on total collapse.

The Black Death is arguably the greatest natural disaster in all of human history. Between 1348 and 1351, the plague killed up to 33 per cent of the entire population of Europe, a total of around 75 million people, and it would strike down millions more in future outbreaks throughout medieval and early modern history. ■

Religious rites were a rarity for the dead and the dying during the plague years. Most of the victims were buried in huge plague pits outside the city walls, many of which are still visible today in Europe.

SPANISH COLONIZATION

THE SPANISH COLONIZATION OF THE AMERICAS RESULTED IN ONE OF THE GREATEST PERIODS OF SOCIAL, HUMAN AND CULTURAL DESTRUCTION IN HISTORY.

The drive for a Spanish empire began roughly around 1469, when Ferdinand V of Castile and Isabella I of Aragon married to bring Spain under the rule of a single monarchical house. With internal politics consolidated, the Spanish now began to look outwards to the formation of an empire.

ENTERING THE AMERICAS

From 1492, when Christopher Columbus made landings on the Caribbean islands, until around 1518, the Spanish consolidated the Caribbean and began pushing outwards into central and southern America. A key element in their colonial expansion was the *conquistadores,* explorer soldiers who became as noted for their cruelty as for their undoubted bravery. Two *conquistadores* in particular stand out for the effect they had on the indigenous American people. One of them was the infamous Hernán Cortés. In 1518, he took a small army up into Mexico, and by 1521 he ➠

The Spaniards introduced firearms into the Americas, weapons which gave them complete superiority over the native Indians.

Above: New developments in transoceanic maritime technology and navigation in the sixteenth century made colonization possible.

had brought about the destruction of the entire Aztec empire, massacring tens of thousands of its people at places such as Cholula and the Aztec capital, Tenochtitlán. In the same way that the Aztec civilization was destroyed, the *conquistadores* of an equally famous explorer, Francisco Pizarro, crushed the Inca empire of Peru during the 1530s, and in 1572 the last of the Inca rulers was beheaded.

COLONIAL DESTRUCTION

Mexico and Peru are but two examples of the excesses of Spanish colonization in the Americas, and military massacres were unfortunately common during the expansion. However, it was not the *conquistadores* themselves who had the most devastating impact on the continent, but the non-indigenous diseases that they introduced, particularly smallpox, measles and influenza. For example, the Aztecs were not only militarily overwhelmed, but were also felled by a smallpox epidemic: around three million died, one-third of the Aztec population. More than 100,000 Incas were killed by the disease in Cuzco, their capital, alone. Estimates for the total disease-related death toll in the Americas between 1500 and 1650 has been placed at around 45 million, which represents around 90 per cent of the indigenous population. The world has rarely seen such enormous cultural destruction since. ∎

The native Indians had once presided over huge internal empires, but most were forced into slavery after the Spanish conquests, with cruel working conditions compounding the effects of introduced diseases.

SLAVERY IN THE AMERICAS

THE TRANSATLANTIC SLAVE TRADE WAS A PHENOMENON AS DURABLE AS IT WAS TERRIBLE, BEGINNING AROUND THE MID-FIFTEENTH CENTURY AND LASTING UNTIL THE 1800S.

It began in 1444, when the Portuguese opened trading relations with the west coast of Africa and began extracting around 800 slaves a year to fill gaps in its domestic agricultural labour market.

HUMAN RESOURCES

By the mid-sixteenth century, however, Spain, Britain and the Netherlands had joined the trade, using African slave labour in the burgeoning European colonies in the Americas. This new market led to a huge expansion in the numbers of slaves required, and about 15,000 a year made the long and harrowing voyage across the Atlantic by the 1600s. Most ended up in the Caribbean or mainland Latin/South America, where they were placed in abusive servitude on plantations (two-thirds of all African slaves would work in sugar plantations) or in mining.

North America received its first batch of slaves in 1619 in Virginia, and what was to be the southern United States ultimately became one of the biggest beneficiaries of the slave trade. Although the imported peoples initially had some on-paper rights under conditions of 'limited servitude', these were ➤➤

> ### KEY FACTS
>
> **An estimated** 10 million African slaves were exported to the Americas from the late 1400s to the early 1800s.
>
> **A low** estimate of fatalities aboard the slave ships is two million dead, although some suggest a figure of up to 10 million.
>
> **Slavery in** the United States is finally terminated following the US Civil War (1861–65).

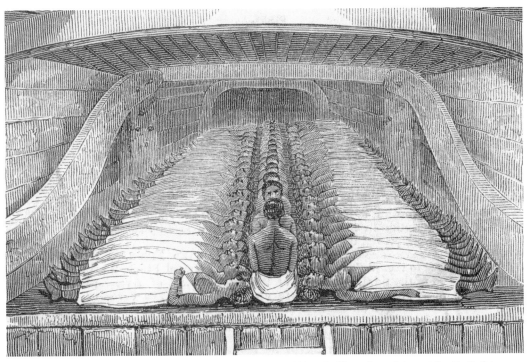

A horrifying though sanitized impression of a slave ship. Such ships would have had limited ventilation, while toilet facilities consisted of little more than a bucket in the corner of the hold.

Above: The king of the Congo welcomes the Portuguese colonizers in the mid-fifteenth century. Congo soon became a major centre of slave exportation, the Europeans making local rulers wealthy through their complicity in gathering and processing slaves.

legally and practically eroded until conditions of full slavery were enshrined in most southern regions.

During the 1700s, Great Britain was the biggest supplier of slaves to the New World, shipping around 50,000 slaves a year. It abolished slave trading in 1807, but the United States retained 893,000 slaves and smuggled in up to 15,000 a year despite Congressional prohibitions on importation from 1808. Only the civil war of 1861–65 overthrew the institution, and even then African-Americans would remain persecuted and segregated in many sectors of American society up until the 1960s.

SHIPS OF DEATH

The crimes committed during the 400 years of the transatlantic slave trade were truly awful. Around 10 million Africans were transported abroad. On the basis of surviving ships' records, it is estimated that some two million died during transit to the Americas; mortality on the slave ships during the mid-1700s ran at around 20–29 per cent. Yet this estimate could be conservative. Those who reached their destination faced a life of unrelenting labour and frequent cruelty, with a short life expectancy. ■

The route to slavery actually began among the African peoples themselves, and many North African rulers actively traded human beings with the colonists and European/American adventurers.

EARLY MODERN DISASTERS 1500 – 1700

The Early Modern period saw a huge expansion in the sum of human knowledge, and a new level of sophistication of science, art, architecture and theology. However, the elemental forces of nature remained just as strong. Great cities were almost wiped out in cataclysmic events, with Lisbon destroyed by earthquake and tsunami in 1531 with the loss of 70,000 lives, and London gutted by fire in 1666. Furthermore, despite the growth of conspicuous wealth within the cities, the majority of the world's population remained as agricultural poor, and they were as vulnerable to natural disaster as ever.

Left: The fire of London in 1666 burnt for three days and destroyed 13,000 houses.

LISBON EARTHQUAKE

MORE THAN MOST OTHER CITIES, LISBON HAS LIVED UNDER THE SHADOW OF SEISMIC DESTRUCTION.

Recent studies have revealed more of the complex interaction of tectonic plates in the region, with the African plate pressing up against Iberia by around 4mm (0.15in) each year. This movement is held under tension rather than being a constant motion, and when the plate finally slips a powerful earthquake occurs.

RECURRING TREMORS

Such is likely to have been the cause of the devastating earthquake of 1531, a time when Lisbon was entering a period of great prosperity owing to Portugal's colonial expansion in Africa, the Far East and the Americas. Earthquakes had struck the city before. In 1344, a quake of magnitude 7 destroyed large parts of the city's infrastructure and severely damaged many of its most prestigious buildings. Almost 200 years later, on 26 January 1531, another earthquake struck, bringing destruction on a potent scale.

The quake measured around 8 on the Modified Mercalli scale. Magnitudes on the Mercalli scale go up to 12, and an earthquake ➤➤

KEY FACTS

- **26 January 1531** – major earthquake hits Lisbon, the previous earthquake having occurred in 1344.
- **More than 1500** buildings are destroyed and 30,000 people killed in the rubble.
- **A tsunami** hits the Portuguese coastline, taking the regional death toll to 70,000.

The tsunami of 1531 hit the Portuguese coastline with immense force. Rather than being a single wave, the tsunami would have formed itself into a huge elevation of the sea level, to submerge entire buildings.

classified as 8 on the scale has a destruction level that is described as follows: 'Houses that are not bolted down might shift on their foundations. Tall structures such as towers and chimneys might twist and fall. Well-built buildings suffer slight damage. Poorly built structures suffer severe damage.' Such a description does little to convey the horror of the event.

BLIGHTED CITY

The impact of the tremor brought down 1500 of Lisbon's houses within a matter of seconds, burying and killing around 30,000 people. Furthermore, the epicentre of the tremor was likely to have occurred offshore, and tsunami waves submerged the Portuguese coastline, pushing the final death toll from the disaster up to around 70,000. It would take years of reconstruction before Lisbon returned to its former glory.

Lisbon, and Portugal, would suffer further cataclysmic destruction from earthquakes and associated tsunami in 1755, when the city was almost obliterated by a seismic event that killed more than 170,000 people (see separate entry, pp 132–135). Observing the 200-year gap between the tremors gives cause for concern that the great city may be revisited by earthquakes in the near future. ■

Above: Portugal was a maritime nation, and its development of a professional navy enabled colonial expansion as far as the shores of India and the Americas. Much of its population was concentrated along coastal strips, a reason why the 1531 death toll was so high.

Lisbon in the early sixteenth century was rapidly becoming one of the world's most powerful cities. This ascendancy is reflected in the number of its spired buildings, which would, unfortunately, prove so vulnerable to both the earthquake and the tsunami.

SINKING OF THE *SÃO JOÃO*

**BY THE MID-1500S, THE WORLD WAS BECOMING A SMALLER PLACE.
THE DEVELOPMENT OF NEW TYPES OF SAILING VESSEL LED TO TRUE
OCEANIC SAILING CAPABILITIES BY THE END OF THE FIFTEENTH
CENTURY, IN TURN FUELLING THE RAPID EUROPEAN COLONIZATION
OF THE NEXT CENTURY.**

The most important of these ship types was the carrack. Carracks
greatly increased the sail power and size of merchant and military
sailing vessels, with some of the biggest examples – such as the
English *Henry Grâce à Dieu* (1514) – weighing around 1500 tons
(1650 tonnes). Such prodigious size enabled the vessels to carry
supplies that would sustain a crew for weeks on a voyage to far-off
colonies. The Portuguese in particular built up a first-class fleet of
carracks to maintain its developing settlements in India, in Central
and South America, and along the African coastline. In 1552, one
of the world's biggest ships was Portugal's *São João Baptista*.

SHIPWRECKED

On 3 February 1552, the *São João* faced a long journey from a Portuguese trading post in Cochin, India,
back to its homeland. Apart from food and water for the 500 people on board, the ship was packed with ➤➤

Portuguese settlements were dotted around the coastline of the African continent by the fifteenth century.

Above: The ship was carrying vast amounts of valuables on its long journey, including Chinese porcelain, this has been recovered from the wreckage.

the kinds of valuables typical of the East – spices, Ming porcelain, beads, precious sea shells. The first half of the journey went relatively smoothly, but on 8 June, as the ship rounded the treacherous southwestern coast of Africa, a huge storm blew up. Soon the *São João's* sails and rudder were wrecked. Floating helplessly, the ship eventually floundered off Port Edward, Natal, and was forced to drop anchor near the coast. While crew and passengers were being transferred to shore, the ship was finally smashed by the storm, with 100 people losing their lives in the sinking.

TERRIBLE WALK

For the 400 survivors, however, the ordeal was far from over. Surrounded by potentially dangerous African coastal tribes, the survivors had no option but to march towards the Portuguese settlement at Delagoa Bay, Mozambique, some 500km (310 miles) to the north. Over the next weeks, they trudged northwards through the blistering temperatures, losing people all the while to dehydration, starvation, disease, wild animals and tribal attacks. Ultimately only 25 people were to reach the safety of Delagoa Bay. The loss of the *São João* provides powerful testimony to the sheer danger, as well as the potential, of undertaking sea travel in the sixteenth century. ∎

The São João *was one of the Portuguese navy's most prestigious vessels, with true transoceanic capability.*

SHANXI EARTHQUAKE

IN TERMS OF LOSS OF LIFE, THE WORLD'S WORST SEISMIC DISASTER OCCURRED IN SHANXI PROVINCE, NORTHERN CHINA, IN 1556.

In the early sixteenth century, Shanxi was a powerful province within the Ming Dynasty, a place particularly known for its trading and financial dealings. Shanxi sits on a seismically temperamental plateau and earthquakes had struck throughout its history. However, nothing in previous years bore comparison with what struck the province, and several other provinces in the region, on 14 February 1556.

REGIONWIDE EARTHQUAKE

On that morning, a cataclysmic earthquake smashed a region in north China some 1295 square kilometres (500 square miles) large. The quake's epicentre was near Hua Shan, Shanxi province. Modern seismological estimates place the magnitude of the earthquake at around 8 on the Richter scale, which describes such an event as follows: 'great earthquake, great destruction, loss of life over several hundred kilometres'. A total of 97 states and counties were hit, causing varying degrees of destruction; however, even as ➤➤

Northern China is a vast hinterland dotted with areas of dense population. Many of the people of China were, and remain, in subsistence lifestyles, and so were acutely vulnerable to the disruptions of a natural disaster.

➤➤

the first shocks subsided it was evident that the death toll from the earthquake would be huge.

FRAGILE HOUSING

Much of the population of northern China lived in poor-quality housing, and in Shanxi province many of the people lived in caves bored into the sides of loess cliffs. Loess is a frangible type of compacted soil deposit, which is easy to dig out (people still live in loess caves in China today), but it is vulnerable to earth tremors and general erosion. In 1556, these caves became tombs for hundreds of thousands of people. It is estimated that around 830,000 people died in the Shanxi earthquake, accounting for a 60 per cent population loss in some areas. The end of the initial quake was far from being the end of the people's sufferings. Fire, a common phenomenon after earthquakes, raged for days in many urban areas, which were also plagued by looting and rioting as social order broke down. Furthermore, aftershocks continued for six months, occurring about two or three times a month and hampering attempts at reconstruction. The region is periodically affected by earthquakes even to this day. ■

Above: In the sixteenth century much of China's housing was located in hilly territory, hence it was extremely vulnerable to landslide.

A picturesque image of classic Chinese cliff housing. From an earthquake survival point of view, such housing could not be more dangerously located or constructed, with much of the structural support coming from long wooden braces.

SMALLPOX AND THE NORTH AMERICAN INDIANS

THE ALMOST TOTAL DESTRUCTION OF THE NORTH AMERICAN INDIAN CULTURE BETWEEN THE EARLY SEVENTEENTH CENTURY AND THE EARLY TWENTIETH CENTURY IS A PARTICULARLY UNPLEASANT ELEMENT OF US HISTORY.

Although military action and forced displacement killed many thousands of North American Indians during this period, disease was by far the biggest killer, smallpox in particular playing a dreadful role in the devastation.

DECIMATED POPULATIONS

Smallpox is an infectious disease that has a 30 per cent mortality rate in its worst forms. Thankfully, it was eradicated in the United States by the early 1950s, but during the preceding centuries it was a disease of serious social impact. The disease is believed to have been imported into the Americas during the late 1400s, first afflicting communities in Central and South America and the Caribbean. The impact in these early stages was itself profound. For example, the native population of Mexico was reduced from 25 million to less than seven million by 1520, and two-thirds ➤➤

KEY FACTS

Smallpox takes hold of North American Indian tribes on the northeastern coast during the early 1600s.

1617–19 – the first major epidemic of smallpox among the Indians decimates the Massachusetts Indians.

Smallpox epidemics over the next two centuries kill more than 500,000 North American Indians.

Native American culture was highly developed by the time the Europeans began to arrive in the New World. Within two centuries the population had been slashed by disease and war, and traditional Indian lands taken over by the colonizers.

➤➤

of all indigenous Puerto Ricans died of the illness around 1515. A century later, smallpox would come to the northeastern coast of what would become the United States, where it had equally devastating consequences.

DECIMATION

British and French colonization of North America began around 1580. The new arrivals brought with them not only aspirations, but also smallpox, against which the eastern Indians had no immunity. In 1617–19, the first major outbreak of smallpox ran through the Indian tribes with ruthless efficiency. It killed 90 per cent of the Massachusetts and Algonquin Indians alone, reducing their population from around 30,000 to fewer than 500. The epidemic irresistibly spread to the west and south, decimating tribes such as the Huron and Iroquois around the Great Lakes. Smallpox would continue to depopulate Indian tribes for the next two centuries. (Thousands of colonists also died from the disease, and death tolls in Europe stood at around 400,000 a year during the 1700s.) Although smallpox was not the only disease to afflict the Indians, it had killed around two-thirds of all Plains Indians by 1800, with around one million Indians having died by the beginning of the twentieth century. ■

When the British first made contact with the Native Americans, the interaction was generally peaceable, and included the exchange of gifts (above). Over time, however, the relationship grew more hostile and more manipulative on the part of the colonizers.

INDIAN FAMINE

**THE TWO FORMS OF DISASTER THAT RESULT IN THE GREATEST
LOSS OF LIFE ARE EPIDEMICS AND FAMINE. THROUGHOUT ITS
HISTORY, INDIA HAS UNFORTUNATELY BEEN VISITED REGULARLY
BY BOTH OF THESE PHENOMENA.**

Historically, a period of around five to ten years separates the
episodes of famine in the country, the famines usually being
precipitated by damaging floods or monsoon rains or, conversely,
by periods of arid drought.

HARROWING ACCOUNTS
One such famine occurred between 1630 and 1631, and the scale
of the disaster was profound – around four million people died
during the nine years of scarcity. A Dutch merchant who was
witness to the events gives a harrowing account of what he saw:
'People wandered hither and thither, helpless, having abandoned their towns or villages. Their
condition could be recognized immediately: sunken eyes, wan faces, lips flecked with foam, lower jaw
projecting, bones protruding through skin, stomach hanging like an empty sack, some of them
howling with hunger, begging alms.' Such was the extent of the famine that human flesh became a
tradable commodity in Indian markets, and the famine continued 'to the point when the country was ➤➤

KEY FACTS

1630–31 – An enormous
   drought-related famine
   causes widespread death
   across India.
The final death toll reaches
   around one million, a quarter
   of which are young girls who
   are deliberately cut off from
   available food supplies.
Cannibalism becomes
   commonplace, with open
   trading in human meat.

A depiction of Dutch traders in India in the eighteenth century. The spread of colonial influence into India meant that famine became an international issue, if only for the cynical reason that the disaster affected trading.

entirely covered with corpses which stayed unburied'. Further, it had a profound effect on the composition of Indian society in the worst-affected regions.

SOCIAL EFFECTS

Traditionally, male offspring were given a far greater value than female offspring in Indian society. A principal reason for this was that females would have to carry a dowry upon marriage, and were therefore seen as an economic burden upon the family, whereas male children brought a dowry into the family, as well as commanding higher wages, and so were an economic blessing. This attitude is still prevalent today in India, but during the famine of 1630–31 it resulted in many starving families diverting all available food away from young females. A full quarter of the one million dead during the famine were girls younger than 14, and once the country recovered from the famine many regions found themselves affected by a severe dearth of eligible women. The seventeenth-century famine was by no means the worst famine to blight India in its long history, and in 1770 Bengal was struck by a famine that killed 10 million people (see separate entry, pp 136–139). ■

Above: Although the 1630–31 famine was drought-related, India also suffered crop failure through flooding. Here a woman takes shelter from monsoon rains.

European trading vessels gather off the coastline of India. The oceanic trade route to India was first opened in the fifteenth century by the Portuguese, who found India a treasure trove of precious metals, spices and cloths. Despite the Europeans deriving such benefit from contact with India, they were often casual or simply unwilling in responding to human disasters on the subcontinent.

ATOCHA

THE STORY OF THE SPANISH GALLEON *NUESTRA SEÑORA DE ATOCHA* IS AMONG THE MOST FAMOUS OF MARITIME DISASTERS, NOT LEAST FOR THE EVENTS WHICH LATER SURROUNDED ITS PARTICULARLY VALUABLE CARGO.

The sinking of the *Atocha* occurred on 6 September 1622, a date by which the Spanish empire was reaching the height of its power. Spain had extensively colonized the Americas, resulting in a constant two-way maritime traffic between the homeland and the colonies. Outgoing journeys took food, weapons, tools and domestic goods to the colonies, while return journeys saw the precious metals and stones mined from the conquered territories.

SETTING SAIL

The *Atocha* was part of the Tierra Firma fleet, which set sail on 24 July 1622 from Cartegna and arrived in Havana, Cuba, around 24 August. At Cartegna, the fleet loaded up with a typical cargo of gold and silver from Peru, Colombia, Ecuador and Venezuela, most of the treasure being put on board the *Atocha* and another galleon, the *Santa Margarita*. On 4 September, the ➤➤

KEY FACTS

- **24 July 1622** – The *Atocha*, part of the Spanish Tierra Firma fleet, sets sail from Cartegna for Havana, departing from Havana for Spain on 4 September.
- **5 September** – the *Atocha* is caught in a hurricane, which drives her onto a reef where she is holed.
- **The *Atocha*** sinks with the loss of 260 lives.

Colonial mariners led hazardous lives, the threat of shipwreck, piracy or battle constantly hanging over their heads.

Atocha and 27 of the vessels pulled out of Havana harbour, destined for Spain. However, disaster began to descend the very next day. A hurricane rolled in over the sea, whipping up mountainous seas and torrential rains.

Above: The Atocha's *gold and silver became the object of salvage hunters until well into the twentieth century. These silver coins were recovered from the wreck.*

LOST AT SEA

The Spanish ships were blown in towards the Florida Keys, and the *Santa Margarita* was grounded on a sandbank in the shallow waters of the coast. Meanwhile, the *Atocha's* crew were struggling to avoid a worse fate. The waves physically lifted the great galleon up and smashed her down onto a reef, punching a hole in the hull before carrying her further to sea, where she would sink.

A total of 260 people went down on the galleon, part of a 550-man death toll among the fleet that day. Five people (three crewmen and two slaves) managed to survive only by clinging to the *Atocha's* mast.

In subsequent history, the human tragedy of the *Atocha* has been overshadowed by the cargo of gold and silver it took down with it, some two million pesos. Only in the second half of the twentieth century was the wreck discovered, and today more than $60 million worth of treasure has been recovered. ∎

The Atocha *represented the transition away from the galley, the old style of warship, as seen here at the right of the picture. Galleys were still heavily reliant upon massed oar power and had limited storage capacity for long journeys. The new generations of carracks and galleons, however, switched entirely to sail power. Fast and manoeuvrable, they had the hold storage to make voyages of several months' duration viable.*

FIRE OF LONDON

IN THE SUMMER OF 1666, LONDON WAS A CITY SIMPLY INVITING A DEVASTATING FIRE. ITS PHYSICAL STRUCTURE WAS A FIREFIGHTER'S NIGHTMARE – CLOSE-PACKED WOOD-FRAMED HOUSES ARRANGED ALONG NARROW STREETS, WITH MANY OF THESE POSSESSING OVERHANGING UPPER FLOORS.

The danger was increased by the strong, dry southeasterly wind that frequented the city, and the summer had been a particularly hot one, making woodwork even more flammable and reducing water levels in rivers and ponds.

THE FIRE STARTS

Many individuals had already recognized the danger of London being devastated by fire. Even the king, Charles II, had expressed concerns at such a possibility. However, all warnings went unheeded and, in the early hours of 2 September 1666, Thomas Farynor, the king's baker, awoke in his house on Pudding Lane (close to London Bridge) to the smell of burning. A fire had started downstairs, and it quickly spread through the house, forcing the family to escape via the roof – a maid stayed downstairs and would die in the fire.

The fire spread to nearby buildings with alarming rapidity. It was unable to cross the London Bridge, but instead concentrated itself in the City of London. By the end of the morning, huge ➻

KEY FACTS

London's layout and wood-framed buildings made the city an acute fire hazard.

Fire starts at 2.00 a.m. on 2 September 1666 in Pudding Lane, and spreads through the City of London by the next morning.

Fire burns for three days, destroying 150 hectares (373 acres) of London.

Panicked citizens of London take to the river Thames in an attempt to escape the fire sweeping through the city. Tradition has given the fire of London a low death toll, but recent historical studies suggest the possibility of thousands of fatalities.

➤➤

Above: Seventeenth-century London's close-packed housing enabled the fire to spread rapidly. Organized firefighting was almost absent, and at the height of the blaze gunpowder charges were used to literally blast down houses and create instant firebreaks.

swathes of central London were in flames. Charles II ordered London mayor Sir Thomas Bloodworth to begin tearing down buildings to create firebreaks, but such measures were ineffective, with the fire leaping more than 32m (100ft) in places.

INFERNO

One day later, and the fire had spread through some of London's most populous districts, such as Gracechurch Street, Cheapside and around the Royal Exchange. St Paul's Cathedral was not spared, and even its lead roof was melted. The rising smoke could be seen by people living in Oxford. The fire kept spreading until 5 September, when a change in wind strength and direction, and an effective use of firebreaks, saw the fire contained, then allowed to burn itself out. The devastation wrought on the structure of London was profound – 150 hectares (373 acres) of city burnt and more than 13,000 houses destroyed. The registered death toll was only four people, but many recent historians consider that the actual toll would have been far higher (possibly into the thousands), as the heat of the flames would have reduced corpses to ash. Indeed, eyewitnesses reported a prevalent odour of burnt flesh. Although many Londoners accused foreigners of starting the fire, there is no real evidence to suggest a cause other than an accident. ■

The fire may have devastated the City of London, but an unexpected bonus of the conflagration was that it killed off much of the city's rat population, thereby helping to reduce the incidences of plague.

THE DROWNING AT ZENTA

THE TRAGEDY THAT OCCURRED AT ZENTA, HUNGARY, ON 11 SEPTEMBER 1697 WAS A CLASSIC INSTANCE OF A MILITARY BATTLE TURNING INTO A HUMAN CATASTROPHE.

The disaster occurred in the context of the Austro-Turkish wars, which plagued eastern Europe between the early sixteenth and the late eighteenth centuries. Vienna had been placed under siege by the Ottoman Turks in 1683, but a combined Austro-Hungarian force broke the siege, then forced the Ottomans on a steady eastern retreat. However, the Ottomans still had an enormous professional military to call upon, and in 1697 a force of around 100,000 Turkish soldiers under Sultan Mustafa II began a determined drive into Hungary in an attempt to claw back the Balkans.

LETHAL PANIC

Mustafa was faced by a much smaller army of around 34,000 soldiers and 16,000 horsemen, but this advantage was countered by the fact that these troops were led by Prince Eugène of Savoy, one of the most capable commanders in the Habsburg army. ➤➤

KEY FACTS

1697 – Ottoman Turks make a powerful offensive into Hungary with around 100,000 troops.

11 September – the Habsburg forces of Eugène of Savoy ambush the Turks as they are crossing the Tisza River.

10,000 Turkish soldiers drown in the ensuing panic, and 20,000 other casualties are sustained in combat.

The battle of Zenta was another victory for the great Habsburg commander Eugène of Savoy, who was given command of the Habsburg armies in 1697 for the fight against the Turks.

Above: Eugène of Savoy (1663–1736) was destined to be a great military leader. He was given his first regimental command at the age of only 21, having distinguished himself in battle.

Although only 35, Eugène had been made commander in chief of the Habsburg forces, as he was a formidable strategist, and on 11 September 1697 he fought his first battle in his new commanding role against the numerically superior Turks.

Mass drowning

The Turks were at this time marching north through Hungary from Belgrade. At one point on their journey, they were forced to cross the deep and fast-flowing river Tisza. They sent the cavalry across first, the infantry preparing to cross behind them on a temporary bridge. Once the cavalry were across, Eugène sprang an ambush. The bridge was quickly destroyed, leaving the cavalry to be surrounded and massacred on the far bank. The Turkish infantry, now faced with a swarming attack, panicked, and this in turn led to one of the largest mass drownings in history. Thousands of men attempted to swim the river at various points to escape the onslaught, and it is estimated that 10,000 men drowned in the process. Soon the river was choked with bodies, with the survivors attempting to hide from the missiles shot at them from the banks. In total, the Turks lost around 30,000 men that day, and two years later they were forced to give up Hungary altogether. ∎

Prince Eugène's masterful ambush threw the Turkish troops into complete panic and disarray.

INDUSTRIAL AGE DISASTERS 1700 – 1900

The major disasters of the eighteenth and nineteenth centuries are generally little different from those of preceding centuries, there being the regular episodes of earthquakes, volcanic eruptions and other natural events. However, enormous population growth during these centuries meant that the death tolls from famine and disease easily climbed into the millions. The technological revolution also brought with it new engines of transportation and warfare, and intensified methods of industrial production and mining. These in turn created a whole new potential for catastrophic events.

Left: The great Chigago fire of 1871 which gave much of the city the appearance of a terrible war zone.

THE EDO EARTHQUAKE

THE CITY OF EDO – MODERN-DAY TOKYO – BEGAN AS A SMALL FISHING VILLAGE.

However, around 1600 the village was transformed when the dominant Japanese noble Tokugawa Ieyasu adopted it as his centre of power, from where he became absolute ruler of Japan in 1603. With all power concentrated upon Edo, the village grew to a town, then into a large city of hundreds of thousands of inhabitants.

SEISMIC DISASTER

The geological region in which Edo was located was, and remains, an area of intense seismic activity. The Japanese islands are sited at the very place where two tectonic plates meet – the Philippine Sea plate and the North American plate. Constantly shifting against one another, these plates have regularly precipitated earthquakes throughout Japan, and in 1703 Edo was struck by one of enormous power. Known as the Genroku earthquake, it struck on 31 December 1703 with a seismic intensity that caused the earth to ripple and brought the fragile wooden housing of Edo crashing to the ground; it is estimated to have been around 8 on ➤➤

KEY FACTS

- **31 December 1703** – Edo is hit by an earthquake measuring around 8 on the Mercalli scale.
- **Combined death toll** from collapsed buildings, fire and tsunami reaches an estimated 150,000.
- **Tokyo is** again badly damaged, with 100,000 killed, by a later earthquake in 1923.

Edo (modern-day Tokyo) in the eighteenth century was one of the most densely populated cities in the world. In the seventeenth century alone, the city grew to a population of around one million, hence the effects of the earthquake were so catastrophic.

WHAT FELL IN A DAY
WE'LL BUILD IN A DAY

JAPAN EARTHQUAKE FUND
FOR METHODIST REBUILDING
A CHRISTMAS OFFERING-1923.

Above: A poster raising funds for reconstruction after the Great Kanto Earthquake of 1923. Japan remains under the cloud of seismic activity.

the Mercalli Scale. Some 6500 people were killed by a resulting tsunami, which struck coastal areas of the Sagami Bay and Boso Peninsula, and estimates of the final death toll from all causes – including the many fires that burned throughout the city following the quake – go as high as 150,000.

Repeated disasters

It would not be the last time in history that the city was to be devastated by earthquake. Known as Tokyo from 1868, the city had a population of more than 3.5 million people by the early twentieth century, and on 1 September 1923 it was hit by another colossal tremor, which became known as the Great Kanto Earthquake. The city was almost entirely wrecked, and once again devastating post-earthquake fires took hold and burned for two days. (A problem with controlling fires in the aftermath of many earthquakes is that the tremors have often fractured water pipes, resulting in there being little available water or water under very low pressures.) The death toll was again enormous, estimated at around 100,000 with a further 40,000 missing (probably incinerated during the fire). In 1995, the city of Kobe was hit by another large earthquake, demonstrating Japan's vulnerability to regular seismic disruption. ■

The impact of the 1703 earthquake was heightened by traditions of housing construction in Japan. Wood and plaster buildings were acutely vulnerable to fire in the aftermath of an earthquake.

LISBON EARTHQUAKE

FOLLOWING THE GREAT EARTHQUAKE OF 1531 (SEE EARLIER ENTRY, PP 94–97), THE CITY OF LISBON SET ITSELF ON A LONG PERIOD OF RECONSTRUCTION.

The 1531 quake had caused huge damage and loss of life, but by the mid-eighteenth century Lisbon was still among the most beautiful cities of Europe.

THE GREAT CITY

The city was replete with magnificent architecture and its population had grown to 275,000. It was also going through a period of intense wealth, the city benefiting from gold reserves discovered in Portugal's Brazilian colony. However, its fortunes were once again reversed by a seismic disaster. On 1 November 1755, at around 9.30 a.m., an enormous earthquake of magnitude 9 radiated out from a point about 200km (120 miles) west-southwest of Cape St Vincent in the Atlantic Ocean. Such was the intensity of the earthquake that the tremors were felt as far north as France and Switzerland, and disturbances in water levels and contours were even noted in Finland. The greatest physical destruction, however, occurred in Lisbon. Much of the city was flattened by the tremors, thousands of people being killed in their ⇒⇒

> **KEY FACTS**
>
> **1 November 1755** – a huge earthquake occurs in the Atlantic Ocean about 321km (200 miles) off the coast of Portugal.
>
> **The city** is devastated by the earthquake, a series of three tsunami that hits Lisbon 30 minutes after the tremors, and a fire that lasts for five days.
>
> **The total** death toll from the earthquake reaches 100,000, more than one-third of the city's population.

The Church of St Nicholas

The destruction of Lisbon was visually documented by the artist Le Bas, who created several engravings of the destruction. Here the Church of St Nicholas is seen completely gutted by the tremors.

collapsed homes or struck by falling rubble. About 30 minutes later, a series of three large tsunami slammed into the Portuguese coastline, wrecking a broad swathe of territory.

MULTIPLE DISASTERS

In the Algarve, waves were measured at more than 30m (90ft). At Lisbon itself, the harbour and downtown areas were inundated, and many people who had taken to boats to escape the earthquake tremors were drowned at sea. Compounding the disaster for Lisbon, those areas not inundated by water suffered from a huge urban fire caused by the upset of hundreds of candles and cooking fires. The fire burnt for a total of five days, during which time some of the most prestigious and beautiful areas of the city were completely gutted. Around 85 per cent of the city was destroyed by the earthquake and resulting fire and tsunami. Nor was Portugal the only country to be affected by the earthquake of 1755: damage and loss of life also occurred in Spain, North Africa and Gibraltar, with the tsunami reaching out as far as Great Britain, Holland and even Barbados. However, the loss of life was most extreme in Lisbon – an estimated 100,000 were killed. Lisbon never fully recovered from the earthquake, and its power in European history was consequently reduced. ∎

Above: Portugal's coastline was battered by three massive tsunami. Here an artist captures the full extent of the devastation, with the assaults from the sea compounding the fires inland and the physical destruction caused by the earth tremors themselves.

Lisbon lies in ruins after being struck by the earth tremors. Coastal areas in seismically active regions are vulnerable not only to tremors, but also to tsunami resulting from the displacement of the ocean floor.

THE GREAT BENGAL FAMINE

THE BENGAL FAMINE OF 1770 STRUCK WITH A COMPLETELY UNEXPECTED SCALE AND INTENSITY.

In 1768, there had been a poor harvest, although enough crops were gathered to prevent the onset of famine. However, in September 1769 a welcome period of rain suddenly stopped and an autumnal drought set in. The rice fields of Bengal, so critical to feeding the population, became in the words of one observer 'like fields of dried straw'. The government of the region was slow to respond, having been warned on numerous other occasions of impending famines which did not then materialize. By 1770, Bengal was in the grip of one of the worst famines in its history.

HELL ON EARTH

Existing stocks of food were soon consumed, and in desperation the people began selling anything of value in order to buy some grain or flour. Once all their valuable agricultural tools, clothing and (for those wealthy enough) jewellery had been sold off, they even, according to one chronologist of the disaster, 'sold their sons and daughters, till at length no buyer of children could be found'. ➤➤

KEY FACTS

1769 – The year sees a long drought and a subsequent failure in key crop harvests.

1770 – Around 10 million people die during the summer of 1770 from starvation and disease.

Depopulation after the famine affects Bengal for the next 15 years.

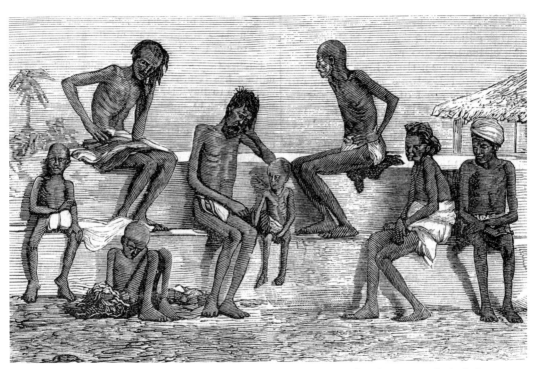

The Bengal famine occurred on such a massive scale that there was little for many people to do except wait for death. Some disaster relief was forthcoming, but not enough to stop millions dying in the streets, homes and fields.

Above: Relief stations could not stop the famine from claiming 10 million lives, many of these from diseases such as cholera and typhus.

As they entered into true starvation conditions, 'they ate the leaves of trees and the grass off the field; and in June, 1770, the Resident at the Durbar affirmed that the living were feeding on the dead.'

RETURNING RAINS

The scale of the disaster was such that rich and poor alike fell foul of starvation or the accompanying diseases. One aristocratic family even had to melt down the family silver to pay for their father's funeral, such was the collapse in the economy. Based on official returns, around 10 million people died in Bengal in the summer of 1770. This death toll is incredible considering that the famine lasted only a period of months. Bengal typically had three harvests – spring, early autumn and December. The rains returned towards the beginning of September, and by the end of the month a good harvest was reaped. The disaster highlighted the precarious nature of existence in the Indian subcontinent at this time. Although the famine ended, Bengal was massively depopulated, and the large proportion of children dead during the famine meant that the population continued to be depleted for some 15 years. ∎

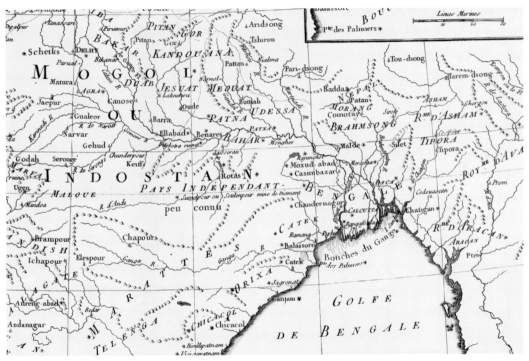

The Bengal region covers an area of around 224,500 square kilometres (86,680 square miles). Today the region is one of the most densely populated areas of the Indian subcontinent, containing around 171 million people.

MOUNT ASAMA ERUPTION

JAPAN HAS MORE THAN 100 ACTIVE VOLCANOES IN ITS TERRITORY; MOUNT ASAMA IS AMONG THE MOST FEARSOME IN TERMS OF THE DEVASTATION IT HAS WROUGHT THROUGHOUT RECORDED HISTORY.

Located in central Japan, Mount Asama sits astride two fronts of volcanic activity, hence its extreme volatility. In May 1753, the volcano began rumbling ominously, and there was an increase in the amount of sulphurous smoke pouring from the summit, which stood at more than 3000m (10,000ft) above sea level. Outputs of ash also rose significantly, so much so that central Japan existed in a constant twilight. This darkening of the sky was already sowing the seeds of a disaster, leading to poor crop growth in the late spring and summer, promising food shortages.

ERUPTION BEGINS

After three months of admonitory signals, Asama finally erupted on 5 August 1783. The initial cataclysmic blast had all the usual ingredients of a major eruption: the air filled with lethal volcanic debris, which shot out across a distance of miles; lava began to pour down into the lowlands; landslides of boiling-hot mud wiped ➤➤

KEY FACTS

May 1783 – Mount Asama in central Japan begins a phase of increased volcanic activity.

5 August – Mount Asama erupts, killing well over 1000 people in the initial minutes of the explosion.

The atmospheric pollution caused by the volcano leads to a devastating famine in Japan, which is responsible 1.2 million deaths.

A striking portryal of the Mount Asama eruption. Note the housing burning along the volcano's slopes and the low light conditions caused by volcanic ash clouds.

Above: The combined effects of massive ash deposits and pyroclastic explosions had a lethal effect on nearby Japanese populations, with housing areas literally razed to the ground.

away entire villages; ash deposits started to suffocate the land of the entire region; pyroclastic flows rushed down the slopes of the volcano, destroying all life in their paths. The initial blast alone killed around 1000 people, and there were many individual instances of tragedy. In the village of Kanbara, for instance, the devastating volcanic emissions killed some 463 people of a village with a population of only 556. The survivors managed to survive the eruption only by ascending to a nearby temple on a small hill, the approach to the temple being via 112 steps. The lava flow reached up to the 102nd step, then thankfully stopped rising.

AIRBORNE THREAT

In common with many volcanic eruptions, the biggest problems emerged with the aftermath. The vast clouds of ash rising out of the volcano blotted out the sun, and temperatures plummeted across northern Japan and stayed low for several months. This effect brought on a widespread crop failure and famine. A total of around 1.2 million people died during the great famine, a huge subtraction from a total Japanese population of some 25 million. ■

Mount Asama continues to be an active volcano, with eruptions as recent as September 2004. The urban centre most threatened by Asama is the nearby resort town of Karuizawa.

FIRE OF MOSCOW

THE FIRE OF MOSCOW IN 1812 WAS A DOUBLE TRAGEDY.

It not only devastated 70 per cent of one of the most spectacular cities in Europe, but also resulted in the destruction of Napoleon Bonaparte's army, which had invaded Russia on 23 June 1812 with 600,000 soldiers. Bonaparte was expecting to meet the Russians early in battle to decide the war, but the Russians instead opted for a retreat in depth, pulling their forces further back into the Russian hinterland and destroying anything of value behind them. Bonaparte's men soon began to starve and suffer from disease, 90,000 men having died by the time the Grande Armée reached Smolensk.

A FRENCH DISASTER

The French did finally draw the Russians into battle at Borodino, where they defeated the enemy, but lost a further 30,000 troops. The Russians kept retreating. On 14 September, 500,000 French troops entered Moscow, having advanced 800km (500 miles) and expecting to receive a surrender and find plenty of food in the Russian capital. Neither was forthcoming. Almost the entire population of Moscow had evacuated the city, taking with them ➤➤

KEY FACTS

- **23 June 1812** – Napoleon invades Russia with a force 600,000 men.
- **14 September** – the French occupy Moscow, but find the city almost deserted. A subsequent huge fire destroys 70 per cent of the buildings in the city.
- **19 October** – the French begin a retreat back from a deserted and incinerated Moscow, with only 20,000 men reaching final safety.

Having been victorious in his previous campaigns, Napoleon suffered his worst-ever defeat during the Moscow campaign, sustaining 95 per cent losses in four months.

much of their food. More disastrously, a huge fire began in the city during the first night of occupation. Whether this was caused accidentally by the French or deliberately by the retreating Russians, the fire swept through the city, killing around 20,000 wounded French soldiers too sick to move and wiping out more than two-thirds of the habitations.

CRUEL RETREAT

For one month, the French attempted to live on in the ruins of the city; however, the cruel Russian winter set in and starvation was costing dozens of lives each day, so Bonaparte ordered the retreat back west on 18 October. Napoleon's retreat from Moscow has gone down as a seminal human and military tragedy. Constantly harassed by Cossack warriors, with almost every man suffering from frostbite and acute hunger, the French retreated while losing hundreds of men each day When the army finally crossed the river Berezina to safety in November, only around 20,000 of the original 600,000 men were left alive. The burning of Moscow, whether an act of Russian sabotage or not, was a moment of cultural destruction that shattered the might of Napoleon's army and condemned hundreds of thousands of Frenchmen to the cruellest of deaths. ■

Above: The fire of Moscow deprived the already exhausted French forces of shelter and food. Although it is arguable as to whether the fire was caused by the Russians themselves, a scorched-earth policy was to be a national tactic in the twentieth century.

Napoleon was of undoubted brilliance as a commander, and inflicted several major defeats upon the Russians; however, his Moscow campaign was defeated by failures in logistics rather than by poor military decisions.

TAMBORA VOLCANO

THE ERUPTION OF TAMBORA ON SUMBAWA ISLAND, INDONESIA, IN 1815 IS A MAJOR GEOLOGICAL EVENT THAT IS POORLY RECORDED IN HISTORY, OVERSHADOWED AS IT IS BY OTHER NINETEENTH-CENTURY ERUPTIONS, SUCH AS THAT AT KRAKATOA IN 1883.

However, the Tambora eruption stands as possibly the most destructive volcanic event in all recorded history, something that temporarily changed the climate of the entire planet.

EARTH-SHATTERING EXPLOSION

Before the 1815 eruption, Tambora was a huge piece of smoking volcanic rock, which may have reached as high as 4000m (13,000ft). On 10 April 1815, the volcano exploded in a truly earth-shattering series of eruptions. A cloud of ash and rock was driven out of the crater to a height of 44km (28 miles). The enormity of the blast can be judged by the fact that the explosion created a caldera which is today around 6.4km (4 miles) across, and the volcano lost 1066m (3500ft) of height. Ash was actually one of the most devastating emissions from the volcano – up to 150 cubic kilometres (34 cubic miles) of the material entered ➤➤

Shipping passes beneath the mushroom cloud emanating from Tambora volcano. The seas around the volcano were heavily polluted by the volcano's ash emissions and also affected by the drop in temperature resulting from reduced sunlight.

➻

the atmosphere. Java, which is more than 800km (500 miles) from Tambora, was covered in a layer of ash 1cm (0.39in) thick. However, the ash was not the greatest initial danger: the first blasts of the volcano threw out tons of lethal rock missiles, and the eruption column collapsed back on itself, causing pyroclastic flows. It is estimated that about 10,000 people were killed on the island itself and the surrounding islands.

VOLCANIC WINTER

Yet the explosion was to have an effect far beyond the immediate vicinity. The ash thrown into the air circled the earth and dramatically reduced the amount of sunlight penetrating through to the ground. Global temperatures fell by around 3 degrees Centigrade, thus creating what became known as 'the year without summer'. The plunge in temperatures caused widespread crop failures and subsequent famines, and it is reckoned that some 85,000 people died as a result of phenomena related to the Tambora eruption. The majority of the dead were confined to the Indonesian islands, but the effects of the volcano were felt in countries as disparate as China, India, Argentina, England and the United States. ■

Above: A photograph taken from the space shuttle Discovery *shows Tambora's caldera, created by the 1815 explosion and measuring 6km (3.7 miles) wide and 650m (2133ft) deep.*

Another shuttle picture, here showing volcanic ash spreading out from eruptions on Papua New Guinea in 1994.

CHOLERA PANDEMIC

CHOLERA, DESPITE BEING A DISEASE WITH CENTURIES OF HISTORY BEHIND IT, IS STILL A KILLER OF THOUSANDS OF PEOPLE EACH YEAR, ESPECIALLY IN THE WAKE OF SERIOUS DISASTERS SUCH AS FAMINES OR FLOODS.

The disease is caused by the bacterium *Vibria cholerae,* which is ingested through contaminated food or water, and it attacks the intestines, causing diarrhoea, vomiting and leg cramps. Those that die from cholera – the process can be rapid, killing in 24 hours in the worst cases – usually do so from massive dehydration.

GLOBAL DISEASE

Cholera epidemics are recorded as far back as the sixteenth century, but the eighteenth and early ninteenth centuries saw the disease at

its most virulent; there have been seven major cholera pandemics since 1817. The first of these pandemics occurred between 1817 and 1823, and like most of the subsequent disease events, it started in India – Calcutta in this case. It then swept through East Asia and the Pacific, the Middle East, and even into southern Russian before the hard winter of 1823–24 stopped it in its tracks.

The pandemic of 1817–23 was overshadowed by what arrived only three years later, another pandemic that ran from 1826–37. Following the previous pandemic, the second also began in India, ➤➤

KEY FACTS

1817–23 – Major Asiatic cholera pandemic stops in southern Russia.

1826–37 – Another cholera pandemic achieves a truly global reach, going from East Asia to the United States.

Millions die in the pandemic, with the disease often killing from dehydration in less than 48 hours.

Public disinfectors prepare to travel through the city streets in a futile attempt to combat the cholera pandemic.

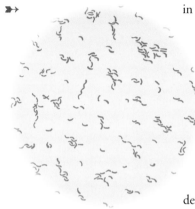

Above: The cholera bacterium, Vibrio cholerae, *is usually tranferred to humans through infected food and water supplies. The disease is particularly prevalent in the developing world, where inadequate sewerage systems allow faecal matter to enter the water supplies.*

in Bengal. This time, however, the disease was going to travel much further, and leave millions dead in its wake. As much as it struck east, it also went west: through Afghanistan and into the Middle East, through Russia, Hungary, Germany, Finland, France and Sweden, crossing the Channel to Great Britain, then the Atlantic to the United States (via infected Irish immigrants) in 1832.

GLOBAL CRISIS

The death tolls were enormous. To cite just four countries, Hungary was one of the worst affected, experiencing 200,000 deaths; Russia lost 197,000 people in 1831 alone; and England and Wales, 21,500 dead. The spread of the disease was facilitated by the huge growth of urban populations during the Industrial Revolution of the 1800s, an expansion which was not matched by an increased sophistication in public sanitation. Furthermore, the military volatility of the period meant that armies transported cholera with them or marched into regions infected with the disease – certain units of the British Army were devastated by cholera during deployments to India and Afghanistan. Although we now understand the mechanism of cholera, it still blights huge regions of the world today. ■

Prior to the twentieth century, cholera prevention measures such as disinfecting (see above) were highly ineffective. The best treatment for a cholera victim was simply constant and quick rehydration.

IRISH POTATO FAMINE

THE IRISH POTATO FAMINE OF 1845–51 REMAINS A SHAMEFUL EPISODE IN BRITISH HISTORY, DESPITE THE FACT THAT THE FAMINE ORIGINATED FROM NATURAL CAUSES.

In the 1800s, the potato was the staple food of around 50 per cent of the Irish population, essential to their subsistence lifestyle. Part of the problem lay in the fact that the British government restricted most farmers to around 2 hectares (5 acres) of land, and potatoes gave a greater yield on these small plots than grain.

CROP FAILURE

During the harvest of 1845, the potato crop was hit by a destructive fungus, *Phytophtora infestans,* the effect of which was to accelerate the decay of the potato once it was infected. After only a few days, the potato became blackened, rotting, slimy and completely inedible. Horrifically, the fungus swept through 50 per cent of the potato crop of 1845, but wiped out almost the entire crop of 1846. The poor of Ireland were plunged into starvation.

The famine in Ireland was of biblical proportions, with a total of around 1.5 million people dead by the early 1850s, starved or killed by associated disease. Contemporary commentators report seeing ➤➤

KEY FACTS

1845–51 – Ireland experiences a catastrophic failure of the potato crop, a food on which 50 per cent of the population rely for existence.

The British government responses are generally uncaring and inadequate, and around one million people die of starvation and disease.

Some three million people emigrate from Ireland to the United States during the famine.

A priest comforts a family during the Irish potato famine. For those who did not die during the famine, emigration to the United States was a desirable option, where people were not faced with the land ownership strictures imposed by the British in Ireland.

Above: The people of 19th century Ireland were acutely dependent upon the potato as a food crop, with meat and other vegetables rare for the rural poor.

skeletal orphaned children hopelessly begging for food, and huge pits for corpses ready for mass burial.

POOR RESPONSE

The response of the British government was appallingly inadequate. At first, Sir Robert Peel's conservative government imported Indian meal, but many of the starving were too poor to be able to afford the food. In 1847, the Whig government provided soup kitchens, but these were inadequate and were then stopped because the government perceived improvements in that year's crop yield. The yield per acre did improve in 1847, but there was less land being cultivated so the famine remained, and was increased again by almost complete crop failure in 1847. To earn a living, many people were channelled into workhouses, but conditions for the weakened people were so appalling that almost 200,000 people died in these institutions.

The Irish potato famine had two important social effects. First of all, it encouraged mass emigration, with around three million Irish people fleeing to the United States between 1845 and 1870. Among those left behind, the memory of the famine fostered an intense Irish nationalism, in turn feeding political violence which lasts to this day. ■

The potato famine brought death on an unimaginable scale to the Irish people. At its height, the famine resulted in parish churches letting the dead go unburied so that they could buy food and clothing for the poor instead of coffins.

SULTANA

THE YEAR WAS 1865, AND THE UNITED STATES WAS ADJUSTING TO THE END OF FOUR YEARS OF CIVIL WAR, WHICH HAD COST THE LIVES OF MORE THAN 600,000 AMERICAN SOLDIERS.

In the South, there were thousands of Union prisoners of war waiting to be repatriated to the North, and a number of steamers were therefore sent down to southern ports to pick them up and take them home.

FATAL REPAIRS

One of these steamers was the *Sultana*, a vessel that was 80m (260ft) long and had a capacity for 376 passengers and crew. On 21 April 1865, the *Sultana* and another steamer, *The Luminary*, set off from New Orleans to Vicksburg to pick up a consignment of released soldiers. However, the *Sultana* was forced to stop for repairs during the journey, having developed a leaking joint in one of her main boilers. The problem was obviously a substantial one, as it necessitated 36 hours of maintenance to patch the leak. (It later transpired that the *Sultana* had experienced problems with the boiler on at least two previous occasions.) ➤➤

KEY FACTS

- **21 April 1865** – Steamer *Sultana* sets sail for Vicksburg to pick up former Union prisoners of war, stopping for boiler repairs on the way.
- **24 April** – The *Sultana* sets sail from Vicksburg up the Mississippi, overloaded with more than 2000 people.
- **27 April, 3.00 p.m.** – The ship's boiler explodes, destroying the ship. Around 1700 people were killed.

The Sultana *seen setting out on its final voyage, evidently overcrowded. The final death toll from the disaster was in excess of more famous shipping accidents such as that of the* Titanic. *The* Sultana *was also carrying 60 horses and mules, and 100 pigs.*

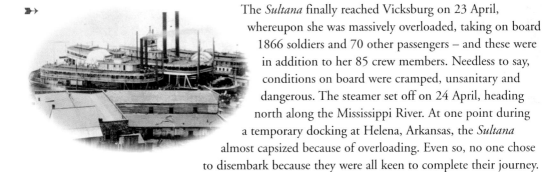

The *Sultana* finally reached Vicksburg on 23 April, whereupon she was massively overloaded, taking on board 1866 soldiers and 70 other passengers – and these were in addition to her 85 crew members. Needless to say, conditions on board were cramped, unsanitary and dangerous. The steamer set off on 24 April, heading north along the Mississippi River. At one point during a temporary docking at Helena, Arkansas, the *Sultana* almost capsized because of overloading. Even so, no one chose to disembark because they were all keen to complete their journey.

BOILER EXPLOSION

Tragedy struck on 27 April, when at 3.00 p.m. the ship's repaired boiler exploded in a huge detonation, killing hundreds of people instantly. One eyewitness described the blast as like 'a hundred earthquakes'. The explosion caused an intense fire aboard the now sinking ship, and those who did not die in the blaze were cast into the rain-swollen waters of the Mississippi. As there were only 76 life preservers and two lifeboats aboard the ship, scores of people drowned. The official death toll was counted at 1238, but the actual figure is more likely to have been in the region of 1700 dead. ∎

The busy port of Vicksburg, from where the Sultana *left for its fatal last journey. The end of the Civil War saw several shipping tragedies, many made worse by the chronic overcrowding of vessels as soldiers sought to make their way home.*

Above: As the Sultana *burns in the background, desperate survivors attempt to swim for the shore. As many men aboard the ship were former prisoners of war, their physical condition was generally poor and many did not have the strength to swim to safety.*

MOBILE MAGAZINE EXPLOSION

MOBILE, ALABAMA, IS AN OLD COMMUNITY. THE TOWN BEGAN LIFE IN 1702 AS A SETTLEMENT ON THE MOBILE RIVER, AND WENT ON TO HAVE A TURBULENT HISTORY CAUGHT BETWEEN THE FORCES OF COLONIAL POLITICS AND CIVIL WAR.

During the American Civil War, Mobile was a Confederate stronghold and was placed under a Union naval blockade by forces of Admiral David Farragut. On 5 August 1864, a large naval battle was fought between Farragut's warships and those of Confederate Admiral Franklin Buchanan. The action resulted in a Union victory, and Mobile fell to the enemy, the Civil War itself ending in April 1865.

LETHAL STORES

In May 1865, Mobile was still very much a military town. The city was heavily garrisoned with Union troops, and large volumes of military ordnance were stored in various locations. On Beauregard Street stood an ordnance depot in which was stacked 200–300 tons (220–330 tonnes) of explosive shells and barrels of gunpowder. Such a large amount of explosives situated in ➺➤

KEY FACTS

April 1865 – The US Civil War ends, and Mobile is garrisoned by Federal troops.
25 May – An ammunition magazine containing around 200–300 tons (220–330 tonnes) of explosives blows up, raining artillery shells across the town and causing a huge fire.
Final death toll reaches around 300.

A dramatic depiction of the Mobile explosion from Harper's Weekly. *Note the two ships destroyed in the harbour, hit by unexploded ordnance thrown out from the explosion.*

Above: Admiral David Farragut (1801–70) was born in Tennessee, but went on to fight for the Union cause in the Civil War.

a densely populated area provided the catalyst for disaster. On 25 May, the ammunition magazine exploded, and a huge column of black smoke and flame shot hundreds of feet into the air.

WIDESPREAD DESTRUCTION

Houses in the immediate vicinity of the depot were blasted flat by the shock waves. Shells were thrown through the air to land and explode hundreds of metres away from the principal explosion. A local newspaper reporter described the ordeal. 'The heart stood still, and the stoutest cheek hailed as this rain of death fell from the sky and crash after crash foretold more fearful fate yet impending. [O]ld and young, soldier and citizen, vied with each other in deeds of daring to rescue the crumbled and imprisoned.'

Following the explosion, which also sank two ships anchored on Mobile River, came a huge and devastating fire, which ran through the northern part of the town. By the time this was finally brought under control, around 300 people had been killed in Mobile. The cause of the initial explosion is still uncertain, although it is most likely it resulted from simple mishandling of the explosives. ■

Mobile, Alabama, was critically affected by the aftermath of the great explosion. Trade in the town dipped for around a decade until redevelopment in the 1880s improved commerce.

ABERGELE RAIL DISASTER

THE ABERGELE TRAIN DISASTER OF 1868 WAS THE UNITED KINGDOM'S FIRST MAJOR FATAL RAIL ACCIDENT.

On 20 August 1868 at 7.30 a.m., the Irish Mail train began its long journey from London to Ireland. The journey would take it from Euston station in London up to Holyhead in North Wales, from where the mail and passengers would be transported to Ireland on the Holyhead ferry. Its passengers were a mix of very rich and middle-class travellers, along with postal workers in the postal carriages. After picking up additional passenger carriages at Chester, the train had four first- and second-class carriages and two postal vans, and by 12.30 p.m. it was heading towards Abergele in Wales.

FREAK ACCIDENT

Ahead of the train at Llanddulas, railway workers were rearranging cargo trucks from the mainline to the sidings. The mainline was on a steep slope, so six cargo trucks temporarily sat on the line, held in place by a brake van. However, other trucks from the sidings were rolled out against the mainline trucks, the brake van ➤➤

A contemporary newspaper artwork depicts the intense fire that engulfed the Irish Mail train near Abergele. Many of the victims were reduced to nothing more than ash and charred bones by the severe heat.

Above: Such was the horrible condition of the accident's victims – only three positive identifications were made – that they were buried in a huge trench, the funeral expenses paid for by the London & North Western Railway Company and the service attended by hundreds.

slipped, and the column of trucks began to roll down the hill towards the incoming train from Abergele. To worsen matters even further, two of the cargo trucks contained 50 barrels of paraffin.

EXPLOSIVE IMPACT

The lack of telegraph connection between Llanddulas and Abergele, and the curving contours of the sea wall along which the mainline passed, meant that the driver, Arthur Thompson, had almost no warning of the approaching disaster. Despite a last-second attempt to throw the train into reverse, the trucks smashed into the Irish Mail and the paraffin exploded, the passenger carriages at the front bearing the brunt of the impact and engulfing fire. Nearby quarry workers made a valiant attempt to control the fire with buckets of sea water, but in a matter of minutes the train was reduced to a twisted and melted wreck. Thirty-three people were killed in the blaze, and such was the intensity of the fire that only three of them could be positively identified. In response to the disaster, the British Board of Trade implemented numerous safety measures, including compulsory telegraph connections between stations. ∎

Rescue workers attempt to find survivors from the Abergele crash. The final death toll could have been significantly reduced had so many passengers not been trapped behind locked railway doors.

THE GREAT CHICAGO FIRE

BY 1871, CHICAGO WAS DEVELOPING AT A FRENETIC PACE.
AS ONE OF THE FASTEST-GROWING CITIES IN THE UNITED STATES,
CHICAGO WAS PACKED WITH CHEAP WOODEN HOUSING WHICH
WAS CONSTRUCTED USING QUESTIONABLE BUILDING STANDARDS,
PRESENTING A SEVERE FIRE HAZARD.

The risk of fire was exacerbated by a three-week lack of the rain.
Indeed, rainfall over the summer of 1871 had been a quarter of
normal levels, so the danger of fire was great.

THE FIRE IGNITES

On 8 October 1871, fire started around the barn of a Mrs
O'Leary on De Koven Street on the west side of the Chicago
River. Fanned by warm, strong southwesterly winds, the fire
quickly took hold, leaping across houses and factories at a
terrifying rate. Soon a large section of the west side was on fire,
and the flames leapt the river to set the east side ablaze, too
(pollution of the Chicago River caused the surface of the water
itself to ignite in many places). Soon many great and famous
buildings were reduced to ashes, including the Tribune Building, ➤➤

The Chicago fire of 1871 gave much of the city the appearance of a war zone. The heavy use of wood in the city's construction, including the use of wood paving in many places, dramatically increased Chicago's incendiary properties.

Above: The flames and smoke of the Chicago fire could be seen from miles away. The riverside areas suffered extremely badly owing to the presence of lumberyards, warehouses full of flammable materials, and the presence of fuel for the ships.

the Palmer and Sherman hotels, and the city courthouse, which collapsed with a roar that was heard more than 1.6km (1 mile) away. The State Street Bridge burned up and allowed the fire to spread to the north side. By this time the city's population was in total panic, a situation worsened by the presence of gangs of looters taking advantage of the social chaos.

QUENCHING THE FIRE

The Chicago fire burned for two whole days before, finally, heavy downpours of rain helped the fire to burn itself out. The fire had destroyed an area 6km (4 miles) long by 1.6km (1 mile) wide. An estimated 300 people had been killed (the official death toll was 125, but many bodies were not found) and 18,000 buildings were lost, leaving one-third of the population homeless, a total of 100,000 people. Legend has gathered around the cause of the fire, the popular version being that Mrs O' Leary's cow kicked over a lantern in her barn, although some evidence points to one Daniel Sullivan setting fire to the barn while stealing milk. However, while there is little dispute as to the source of the fire, the actual cause may never be known with certainty. ■

Survivors of the Chicago fire inspect the tremendous damage done to the city's infrastructure.

FIJI MEASLES EPIDEMIC

FROM THE FIFTEENTH TO THE NINETEENTH CENTURIES, THE WORLD UNDERWENT A TOTAL TRANSFORMATION THROUGH COLONIZATION AND THE TRAVEL ENABLED BY IMPROVEMENTS IN MARITIME TECHNOLOGIES AND NAVIGATION.

Contact with foreigners, however, precipitated some of the greatest epidemiological disasters in history, as was illustrated among the population of Fiji in 1875.

IMPORTING DISEASE

European trade interest in Fiji began in the early 1800s, the islands offering a source of sandalwood and sea cucumbers. In return, the Fijians acquired Western weaponry, which facilitated a long period of clan warfare and social unrest. An ingress of English missionaries and traders in the mid-1800s signalled an increased British involvement in the island, and Fiji became a crown colony on 10 October 1874. Before 1875, the disease of measles – common in Europe – had never touched the shores of Fiji. The Fijian king, however, in preparation for the official handover of the islands to the British, visited Australia on government business, ➤➤

Fiji appeared as a place of tropical idyll to the British, who colonized it in 1874. The British governor Sir Arthur Gordon attempted to keep Fiji's self-sufficiency through growing plantation crops, but the conditions on the plantations unfortunately made them breeding grounds for disease.

Above: Before the 1870s, Fijian rulers had traditionally been hostile to foreign intruders – one British clergyman attempting to convert the locals in the 1850s was ordered to be killed and eaten, and foreign settlements were attacked and burned.

taking with him his young son. During this trip, the son contracted measles, as did one of the king's servants, and these two carriers then transported the disease back to their home islands. The king himself was also probably affected, for on his return to Fiji he convened a conference of all the tribal chiefs of the islands, who as a consequence took the disease out to every corner of Fiji.

NO IMMUNITY

The effect was disastrous. Measles ran through Fijian society unhindered, and was a fatal illness owing to the lack of indigenous immunity. The illness spread at such a rate that the sick and dying soon threatened to outnumber the healthy, this in turn restricting the numbers available to implement health-care measures. (It is noteworthy that 147 natives under British military command all contracted the disease, but suffered only 6 per cent fatalities thanks to British medical care, whereas the rest of the population had a 26 per cent fatality rate). One third of the islands' 150,000 people died of the measles, retarding the islands' economic and social growth for decades to come. ∎

Fijian tribal societies were acutely vulnerable to disease. Not only did the peoples live in close-knit groups with poor sanitation and hygiene, but also their relative isolation from outsiders meant that the people had poor immunity to non-indigenous illnesses.

FAMINE IN CHINA

DURING THE NINETEENTH CENTURY, THE POPULATION OF CHINA WAS BEGINNING A SEEMINGLY INEXORABLE RISE.

In the sixteenth century, the population of this vast land had stood at around 150 million, but by 1850 this figure had risen to 450 million. Many of these people were concentrated around the great waterways such as the Yellow and Yangtze rivers, using the water to fuel basic subsistence agriculture. Hampered by floods or, conversely, regular periods of drought, the millions of poor Chinese eked out a precarious living in a country with little organized infrastructure.

DROUGHT AND FAMINE
Between 1876 and 1879, all five provinces of north China were hit by one of the most prolonged droughts in recorded history, in which an estimated 13 million people died. There were three main reasons for the high death toll: first, an obvious lack of water, which led to death through dehydration, although this was actually the least powerful of the causes; secondly, famine induced through crop failure and subsequent starvation; and thirdly, and ➤➤

The famine of 1876–79 decimated huge areas of China, with a disproportionate effect upon children.

➤➤

Above: Waterways became major highways for the transportation of disease during the famine, as they were often used for corpse disposal.

probably the biggest killer, epidemics of disease resulting from drinking poor-quality water, eating dangerous foods (grass mixed with clay became a common food, resulting in dysenteric illnesses), general weakened immunity and also the growing presence of thousands of corpses (piles of bodies were simply dumped in open grave pits).

Whatever the cause of death, China descended into horror. European travellers through the affected areas speak of dozens of skeletal bodies lying by the sides of the roads, being eaten by fattened wolves. One English missionary reported, 'the eating of human flesh is a regular thing', and there were even reports of human flesh being traded in markets. Relief efforts were hampered by the appalling conditions of China's road network, but Western organizations did bring some relief, particularly from the United Kingdom and United States, before crop levels recovered around 1880. ∎

A vivid contemporary cartoon strip depicting the terrible effects of the famine in China. The strip shows, among other scenes, images of cannibalism and of suicide as differing responses to the starvation conditions.

KRAKATOA

**THE ERUPTION OF KRAKATOA IN 1883 IS ONE OF THE MOST
VIOLENT GEOPHYSICAL EVENTS IN WORLD HISTORY.**

Krakatoa was located in the waters of the Sunda Strait in Indonesia,
set between the islands of Java and Sumatra. Over its one-million
year history, it first evolved into a cone-shaped mountain towering
1828m (6000ft) above sea level, before eruptions reduced it to a
series of minor cones and features that projected above the water
line and together formed a volcanic island. By 1883, its maximum
height above sea level was 813m (2667ft).

HUGE BLAST

In May 1883, Krakatoa began to erupt after a quiet period of
nearly 200 years. A large explosion was recorded on 20 May, and
there were further eruptions on 19 June, but although these were significant disturbances none
compared with what was to follow. On 26 August at 1.00 p.m., Krakatoa began to make a series of
increasingly violent explosions, one propelling an ash cloud 27km (17 miles) high. Then, on 27
August at 10 a.m., the island virtually disintegrated in a truly awesome eruption. The noise of the
blast was heard as far away as Rodriguez Island in the Indian Ocean, 4653km (2891 miles) away from
Krakatoa. A huge pillar of ash 80km (50 miles) high reached into the atmosphere, and the pressure ➤

Ship crews around Krakatoa reported that pumice deposits up to 3m (10ft) thick were floating on the waters.

➤➤

Above: The steamer Berouw *after being carried by a tidal wave into the jungle at Telokh-Betang, Sumatra. As an illustration of the power and force of the tsunami, blocks of coral weighing as much as 600 tons were thrown ashore.*

waves of the blast were picked up by every barograph on the planet, with some even recording the travel of the air waves five days after the detonation occurred. The explosion also threw out 21 cubic kilometres (5 cubic miles) of rock, and more than 800,000 sq km (300,000 sq miles) of territory were affected by ash fallout. Indeed, so thick was the pumice floating on the water that patches were large enough to support people and stop ships. Spectacular sunsets were reported around the world, and global temperatures were reduced by 1.2°C.

WIDER EFFECTS

Krakatoa's eruption would have just been a incredible spectacle had it not triggered enormous tsunami, which reached heights of around 40m (120ft). Tidal increases were reported as far away as South America, and the coastlines of Java and Sumatra were hit by devastating waves that killed more than 36,000 people. Little remained of Krakatoa after the eruption, and what land stayed above water was so choked with ash that it could not support any life. Volcanic activity in the region continues to this day, although the prospects of another Krakatoa-size blast seem thankfully remote. ■

This artistic impression of the Krakatoa blast clearly shows the fallout from the underside of the ash cloud.

DISASTERS OF A NEW CENTURY 1900 – 1945

The first half of the twentieth century was dominated by two global disasters in the form of two world wars. These wars killed more than 70 million people, with World War II accounting for far more civilian deaths than military fatalities. Human activity causes an alarming high proportion of the world's calamities in this period, from Stalin's purges to the Japanese army's massacre in Nanking in 1937. Yet the wars did not leave the world exempt from other forms of disaster. For example, society was still reeling from the effects of World War I when the influenza pandemic of 1918–1919 struck, killing more than 70 million people.

Left: The resulting famine and disease caused by the China flood of 1931 killed around 3.7 million people.

MARTINIQUE VOLCANO

AT THE START OF THE TWENTIETH CENTURY, THE SMALL ISLAND OF MARTINIQUE IN THE FRENCH CARIBBEAN WAS A FASHIONABLE AND POPULAR HOLIDAY DESTINATION FOR EUROPEANS AND AMERICANS, WHICH GAVE THE ISLAND PROSPERITY AND STYLE.

Yet the island had a forbidding presence, the volcano of Mount Pelée, which overshadowed the city of St Pierre, home to 20,000 of Martinique's citizens.

SIGNS OF DISASTER
In January 1902, Mount Pelée began to show signs that it was reawakening, as its emissions of sulphur vapour increased dramatically. By April, the island was already beginning to feel minor earth tremors and show some of the classic signs of an impending eruption. Small eruptions were recorded from 23 April, the waters in the crater lake became scaldingly hot, and animals and insects living on the volcano descended to lower ground (50 people died from snakebites alone).

The population of St Pierre should have been moving away from the city, but politics was to keep them there. Local government **➺➜**

KEY FACTS

January 1902 – Mount Pelée shows signs of increasing volcanic activity, with minor eruptions taking place from 23 April.

5 May – large volcanic mudslide travels down the side of the volcano, killing 23 people.

8 May – Mount Pelée erupts, and a pyroclastic flow wipes out St Pierre, killing almost 28,000 people.

The pyroclastic flows that hit St Pierre consisted of dense mixtures of rock fragments and superheated gases, these travelling in clouds at hurricane-force speeds of 100km/h (60mph).

Above: Martinique was an idyllic place for settlers, and the French began colonizing the island in 1635. The life of the island was totally transformed by the eruption of 1902, and Martinique subsequently struggled to rebuild itself for the tourist industry.

elections were due to be held on Martinique on 11 May, so the governor, Louis Moutett, and his officials went to great lengths to reassure the public that there was absolutely no need for evacuation and that they were perfectly safe. The population of St Pierre even swelled to around 28,000, as people purposely went to the city on the assurances of safety. It was to prove a tragic deceit.

OBLITERATED CITY

On 5 May, a huge, red-hot mudslide ran down the side of the volcano as the rim of the crater gave way, killing 23 workmen in a local rum distillery. The resulting fissure pointed directly towards St Pierre, some 6.4km (4 miles) away; then, on 8 May at around 7.30 a.m., the volcano erupted with an awesome blast. From the fissure came a furnace-hot pyroclastic flow of molten rock and superheated gas. It reached St Pierre in only 60 seconds, wiping the city off the face of the map. Of the 28,000 inhabitants, only two survived, with most being killed by burning and asphyxiation. More eruptions were to follow throughout the year, costing another 1000 lives. The eruption awoke the scientific world to the phenomenon of pyroclastic flows, which were far deadlier than any lava emissions. ∎

St Pierre was razed to the ground by the pyroclastic flows from Mount Pelée, with only two people surviving from a population of nearly 30,000; the blast was 40 times stronger than that of the Hiroshima bomb. Martinique's capital was subsequently moved to Fort-de-France, and St Pierre never regained its former glory.

GENERAL SLOCUM DISASTER

NEW YORK IN THE EARLY 1900S WAS ALREADY A MELTING-POT CITY OF NUMEROUS CULTURES AND ETHNICITIES.

Set on the Lower East Side was Kleindeutchland, a concentration of nearly 100,000 German immigrants living in a community that would not have looked out of place in Munich or Frankfurt.

TRAGIC PASSENGERS

The Kleindeutchland also had a lively religious life, and at the end of the Sunday School year in 1904, 1300 children and worshippers of St Mark's Lutheran church on East 6th Street gathered together for a celebratory outing. The date was 15 June, and the boat they boarded at Locust Grove on Long Island Sound was the steamer *General Slocum*.

The *General Slocum* set off up the East River with its lively cargo at 9.30 a.m., the decks packed with excited children. Then, as the ship tracked past 90th Street, a fire broke out in a forward storage room. Although the blaze started small, the ship's poorly trained crew, armed with rotted fire hoses, could not contain it, and within 10 minutes it had developed into a major ship fire. When ➥

KEY FACTS

- **15 June 1904** – 1300 people, mostly children, board the steamship *General Slocum* for a journey up the East River, New York.
- **Fire breaks** out on board ship. The captain decides to sail for North Brother Island, 1.6km (1 mile) away.
- **The ship** is destroyed by fire, and 1021 people either die on the ship or drown after jumping overboard.

The General Slocum *is here seen half-submerged and wreathed in clouds of smoke from the fire. The largest percentage of fatalities resulted from drowning rather than the flames and smoke.*

Above: Many of the children who formed such a large percentage of the General Slocum's *passengers that fateful June day had never had the opportunity to learn to swim.*

Captain William Van Schaick was finally informed, he made the worst possible decision. Instead of docking immediately – Schaik feared igniting oil storage containers along the shore – he chose to make a full-speed run towards North Brother Island a mile away. The increased speed whipped the fire into an inferno.

PANIC

The passengers became frantic with terror, with children and adults dropping over the side of the steamer to avoid the flames. There most of them drowned – the lifeboats had been wired down and all the life jackets had rotted away (furthermore, many of the young city dwellers could not swim). Others burned to death inside the ship; the ship's coating of fresh paint acted as a pyro-accelerant. The *General Slocum* did reach North Brother Island, but as an inferno. Rescue vessels had followed the ship, but mostly they sailed through hundreds of bobbing corpses, a voyage that left many rescuers traumatized for the rest of their lives. The final death toll was 1021. The victims were displayed in open coffins for identification, and leaders from around the world sent heartfelt condolences to the city. It was the worst disaster in New York before the attacks on 11 September 2001 against the World Trade Center. ■

Of the 1021 people who died during the General Slocum disaster, 61 were unable to be identified, either due to burns or because they remained undiscovered in the water for some days. They were buried in a large communal pit.

SAN FRANCISCO EARTHQUAKE

THE SAN FRANCISCO EARTHQUAKE OF 1906 STANDS AS THE UNITED STATES' GREATEST GEOLOGICAL DISASTER.

In 1906, the population of the city was around 400,000, a population precariously balanced upon the San Andreas fault.

POWERFUL TREMORS

On 18 April 1906, at 5.12 a.m., the city was awakened by a powerful earth tremor, which quickly subsided. Twenty seconds later, all hell broke loose as the San Andreas fault ruptured along 430km (267 miles) of its length, with the epicentre concentrated on the city itself. The earthquake lasted for about 45 seconds, with the ground being displaced 6m (20ft) in places, and the magnitude of the quake registered around 7.7 on the Richter scale. In the 45 seconds it shook, the city of San Francisco was wrecked: buildings collapsed; water mains split apart; people died both in their homes and out in the streets, where they were killed by lethal blocks of falling rubble. Yet although huge devastation occurred in less than one minute of tremors, the disaster was to be prolonged over three days by the huge fires that broke out across the city, fuelled by fractured gas lines. The fire burned for a total of three days, during which time it incinerated an area of around 12.1 square kilometres (4.7 square miles) before it was finally brought under control. ➤➤

> **KEY FACTS**
>
> **18 April 1906**, 5.12 a.m. – San Francisco experiences an initial tremor, followed 20 seconds later by a massive 45-second earthquake measuring 7.7 on the Richter scale.
>
> **The earthquake** and a resulting three-day fire kill around 3000 people, leave 225,000 homeless and cost $400 million.

San Francisco's precipitous streets aided the passage of the fire that resulted from the earthquake, as the flames travelled more easily along uphill routes. This photograph was taken by Arnold Genthe from the top of Sacramento Street and clearly shows the fire advancing towards the onlookers.

After the fire came the grim task of damage assessment. The total number of buildings destroyed was 28,188. Revealingly, only 3168 of that figure was accounted for by brick-built houses, the remainder of the total indicating how appallingly vulnerable wood-built houses were to an earthquake. The property damage had a financial cost in 1906 dollars of $400 million. More seriously, more than half of the city's entire population – 225,000 people – were rendered homeless. They, however, could be classed as the lucky ones. Although precise figures for the final death toll are difficult to ascertain, it is likely that around 3000 people died during the earthquake and subsequent fire.

Above: San Francisco's physical structure was severely destabilized by the earth tremors, particularly among those buildings located close to the fault rupture. However, the greatest portion of the destruction visited upon the city came from the resultant fire.

FUTURE TREMORS?

Today, the city of San Francisco remains astride the San Andreas fault, which according to most scientists has a typical main eruption cycle of once every 200 years. However, significant tremors may occur well before 2106 and, with San Francisco's population at 750,000, the consequences of another major earthquake could be even more profound than the 1906 event. ∎

The earthquake was caused by a rupture along the northern end of the San Andreas fault, extending for 430km (267 miles).

MONONGAH MINING DISASTER

By the beginning of the nineteenth century, the United States already had a burgeoning coal-mining industry, albeit a dangerous one.

Workers were routinely killed in roof falls, gas explosions or machine accidents, but nothing prepared the country for what occurred on the morning of 6 December 1907.

UNDERGROUND EXPLOSION

The location was Monongah, West Virginia, the site of the Marion County mines. Coal production was high at the mine, the miners tapping into the rich Pittsburgh No. 9 Seam, which extended under three states (Ohio, West Virginia and Pennsylvania). On the morning of the 6th, safety officer Lester Trader descended the mine to check for concentrations of methane gas – or 'black damp', as it was called. He reported that it did not exceed average levels, and so it was that 380 miners descended into the No. 6 and No. 8 mines of the Fairmont Mining Company. The mines had been connected by work tunnels, a fact that would have tragic consequences for the men.

At 10.28 a.m., the residents of Monongah were going about their daily business. Suddenly, a thunderous detonation rattled the houses, the blast being sufficient to blow in windows several miles ➤➤

> ### KEY FACTS
>
> **6 December 1907** – 362 miners killed in an enormous underground explosion in No. 6 and No. 8 mines of the Fairmont Mining Company, Monongah, West Virginia.
>
> **Explosion caused** by the build-up of methane gas, which was then ignited by causes unknown.
>
> **More than 1000** miners killed in US mining accidents between 1907 and 1909.

Miners and relatives gather at the pit head to await news of their colleagues and loved ones underground.

Above: A miner injured by the Monongah explosion. The Monongah disaster focused national attention on the dangers of the mining industry, where a high risk of both injury and death was rewarded with wages as low as $3 per week.

away. It was obvious straightaway what had happened – the mine had exploded. The impact was instantaneous: 362 miners were killed, the flames and blast channelling themselves through the connecting tunnels to magnify the disaster. As for those who did not die in the blast, it was later assumed that they had been poisoned by the build-up of methane.

ANXIOUS WAIT

On the surface, a rescue/body-retrieval operation was put into action, hampered by the cave-ins and fire caused by the explosion. The work itself was dangerous, with numerous miners being overcome by the lethal concentration of gases. It would take several weeks before all the bodies of the miners were disinterred, a truly awful time for the hundred of relatives who waited around the mine, hoping vainly that their loved one might have survived. More than 250 wives lost their husbands, and suddenly had to find the means to support their children.

The Monongah mining disaster focused attention on the increasingly high accident rate in US mines. Despite the fact that the cause of the blast was never precisely determined (although methane was judged the most likely culprit), the government steadily introduced more safety legislation in mining. ■

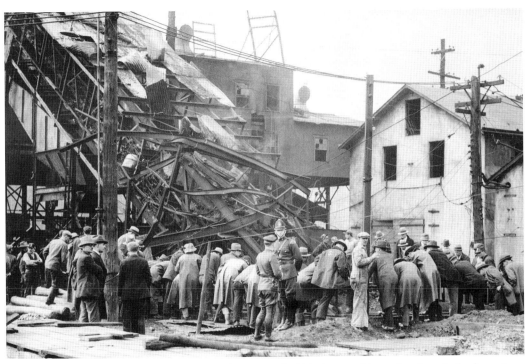

Several mining disasters occurred in the United States after Monongah, this is the scene of devastation after a similar disaster in 1929 at Parnassus in Pennsylvania.

TRIANGLE SHIRTWAIST COMPANY FIRE

THE DISASTER AT THE ASCH BUILDING IN NEW YORK CITY IN MARCH 1911 STANDS AS ONE OF THE WORST INDUSTRIAL ACCIDENTS IN US HISTORY, A TRAGEDY COMPOUNDED BY GROSS HUMAN NEGLIGENCE AND EXPLOITATION.

The seamstresses and machine operators of the Triangle Shirtwaist Company were almost all dreadfully paid immigrants, most in their teenage years. Factory conditions were hot and poorly ventilated, and, crucially, only one rickety fire escape led out of the building.

IGNITION

On 25 March 1911, a fire started on the eighth floor of the 10-storey building, probably caused by a cigarette being dropped onto oily rags. The eighth floor was packed with cloth bins, loose rags and hanging garments, and the fire flashed around the 32m (100ft) square floor with terrifying pace. The building's physical structure was soon ablaze, the flames pouring up into the ninth floor, where the terrified girls either burnt to death or attempted to make a desperate escape using the company elevators or the fire escape. Those who fled up from the tenth floor onto the roof endured the terrible spectacle of seeing terrified employees on the floor below throw themselves to their deaths rather than burn – by the time the fire ⮕

KEY FACTS

25 March 1911 – Fire breaks out on the eighth floor of the Asch Building, used by the Triangle Shirtwaist Company.

145 employees burn to death or jump to their deaths from the upper floors, with most of the fatalities concentrated on the ninth floor.

The Triangle Co. owners are put on trial for manslaughter, but are acquitted. They later make civil settlements.

Firefighters direct their hoses up towards the eighth and ninth floors of the Asch Building.

➤➤

stopped, more than 30 corpses would be piled up on the sidewalks. Thankfully, those who made it to the roof were rescued by workers in other offices and factories who rushed to their aid with ladders. Those still inside the ninth floor made increasingly desperate attempts to escape, even throwing themselves down the lift shafts to land on the roof of the descending elevators, which would soon stop working. Finally, the fire escape also collapsed.

PUBLIC OUTCRY

Once the firefighters arrived, the blaze was controlled in only 18 minutes. By that time, however, 145 people were dead. Fire officers saw the charred, skeletonized remains of the girls, many of them burnt where they had stood, paralysed by fear. The disaster provoked a public outcry, and the owners of the company – Isaac Harris and Max Blanck – were put on trial for manslaughter. A cornerstone of the prosecution case was that numerous witnesses claimed that a main ninth-floor door was locked, allegedly because Harris and Black were fanatical about preventing theft of items. After an eight-month trial, however, Harris and Black were acquitted, although 23 civil cases were subsequently brought against them. When they finally settled the case on 11 March 1913, they had paid damages of only $75 per life lost. ∎

The immigrant community formed a large percentage of the clothing manufacture industry in the first decades of the twentieth century. They suffered from low wages, few holidays and poor working conditions.

TITANIC

THE STORY OF THE RMS *TITANIC* IS POSSIBLY THE MOST FAMOUS, AND THE MOST ROMANTICIZED, DISASTER IN WORLD HISTORY.

Although there have been maritime disasters that have far eclipsed the *Titanic* in terms of death toll, few shipping accidents have contained the movie-friendly ingredients of the *Titanic* tragedy. Yet looking past the mythologies, there is no denying the awfulness of what occurred on 14 April 1912 in the Atlantic.

THE UNSINKABLE LINER

The *Titanic* was one of three superliners laid down by the White Star Line at the beginning of the twentieth century. The ship's specifications were awesome for the time – 260m (853ft) long, 46,329 tons (51,069 tonnes) in weight, with nine decks and a passenger and crew complement of 3511 people. It was famously proclaimed as being 'practically unsinkable' thanks to 15 watertight bulkheads, which could be closed electronically in the event of flooding. The ship was also the height of luxury, which explains why its maiden voyage from Southampton to the United States under the captaincy of Commodore Edward J. Smith ➤➤

KEY FACTS

10 April 1912 – *Titanic* sets sail from Southampton on its maiden voyage from Southampton to New York.

14 April – *Titanic* hits an iceberg in the North Atlantic, and begins to sink.

Only 700 passengers evacuate to safety, and the *Titanic* sinks around 2.20 a.m. on 15 April with the loss of 1600 lives.

The Titanic *was a truly magnificent vessel, yet its provisions of safety equipment and lifeboats were completely underestimated. It carried only 20 lifeboats on board, the largest of these being 14 wooden boats each with a total capacity of 65 people. There were several thousand personal flotation devices, but these could not prevent people dying of hypthermia in the water.*

Above: Captain Edward Smith has a poor reputation in history owing to his role in the Titanic *disaster, particularly through allowing lifeboats to depart only partially filled. That said, Smith had not been provided with sufficient lifeboat capacity.*

attracted 329 first-class passengers, who together had a combined wealth of $500 million.

RIPPED OPEN

The *Titanic* set sail on 10 April, sailing first for Cherbourg and Queenstown, before heading out into the Atlantic. On 14 April, while cruising through the North Atlantic, the *Titanic* received radio warnings of ice floes ahead, but no change was made to either course or speed. At 11.30 p.m., a lookout reported a large 'iceberg straight ahead'. Evasive manoeuvres could not prevent the ship striking the ice, which tore open a large section of hull and destroyed six of the watertight bulkheads. It quickly became apparent that the unsinkable ship was indeed going down, and while distress signals were broadcast the evacuation began. Here lies the root of the tragedy. Following outdated 1894 shipping legislation, the *Titanic* had only enough lifeboats for 962 people, and during the erratic evacuation many of the lifeboats left the decks without their full capacity. Around 700 passengers were carried away by 2.20 a.m., when the great ship rose in the water, split in half and sank. Some 1600 people died in the freezing Atlantic waters, the lucky survivors being picked up by the liner *Carpathia*. It remains a dreadful event in maritime history. ∎

It is an irony that Smith chose a more southerly route of crossing the Atlantic to avoid icebergs. However, he did not slow the ship when ice warnings were received, and at 21 knots there would have been little time to avoid an iceberg emerging from the night.

LUSITANIA

THE SINKING OF THE *LUSITANIA* DURING WORLD WAR I IS ANOTHER AWFUL EXAMPLE OF HOW CIVILIANS CAN BE TRAPPED BETWEEN WARRING NATIONS.

The *Lusitania* first took to the seas on 7 June 1906. Weighing some 32,000 tons (35,274 tonnes), it was a spacious cargo and passenger vessel, its main sea route being between England and the United States.

U-BOAT ATTACK

During the first year of World War I, there had been a steady escalation of German U-boat attacks on Allied merchant vessels. The *Lusitania* was given a warning by the British Admiralty to avoid the seas off southern Ireland, and to maintain zigzag manoeuvres to throw off possible enemy targeting. Indeed, before she set sail from New York to Liverpool on 1 May 1915, German warnings against merchant vessels had been published in US newspapers. However, the *Lusitania*'s captain, William Turner, was confident that the vessel's speed would give the ship all the safety it needed, so he ignored the warnings. ➤➤

KEY FACTS

1 May 1915 – the *Lusitania* sets sail from New York to Liverpool, having ignored warnings of German U-boat activity.

7 May – The *Lusitania* is torpedoed by a German U-boat off the coast of southern Ireland.

A huge secondary explosion causes the *Lusitania* to sink in only 18 minutes with the loss of 1198 lives.

The Lusitania – *240m (785ft) in length and 27m (88ft) in beam – prepares to set out on voyage.*

Above: This photograph perfectly captures the opulence of the Lusitania, *the interior of the ship being created by designer James Millar. The great vessel was launched on 7 June 1906, and such was her attraction that 20,000 people gathered to watch the event.*

The *Lusitania* pulled out from New York with 1198 people aboard. On 7 May, the ship was steaming off Queenstown, Ireland, when it was spotted by German U-boat *U-20*. It fired a single torpedo, which hit the *Lusitania* amidships and exploded. This resulted in a catastrophic ingress of water and also an enormous secondary explosion, which ripped the boat apart and sent her to the bottom of the ocean in only 18 minutes. In those 18 minutes, 1198 people were killed.

CONTROVERSY

The cause of the secondary explosion has been surrounded by much speculation. There are two likely explanations. The first is a boiler explosion, caused the cold seawater hitting the red-hot boilers. The second is the fact that the *Lusitania* was secretly carrying around 173 tons (109 tonnes) of artillery and rifle ammunition; the detonation of this would certainly have caused the destruction of the vessel. Whatever the case, the sinking of the *Lusitania* drew an enormous public outcry, particularly in the United States, which had lost 128 citizens aboard the ship. In 1917, the United States entered World War I on the side of the Allies, and cited Germany's U-boat war as one of the reasons for joining the hostilities. ■

A horrifying impression of the Lusitania *slipping beneath the waves. The captain of the German U-boat that sunk the* Lusitania, *Kapitänleutnant Walther Schwieger, had already sunk three other ships in the previous two days.*

INFLUENZA PANDEMIC

BETWEEN 1918 AND 1919, THE WORLD WAS GRIPPED BY A DISEASE WHICH KILLED AN ESTIMATED 70 MILLION PEOPLE, MAKING THE PANDEMIC SECOND ONLY TO THE BUBONIC PLAGUE OF THE MIDDLE AGES IN TERMS OF VIRULENCE AND DEATH TOLL.

The influenza pandemic had its origins in the trenches of the Western Front during the last year of World War I (1914–1918). A severe flulike illness started to afflict Allied soldiers in France in the spring of 1918, although they usually recovered in less than two weeks. However, by midsummer the symptoms of the illness had intensified, causing pneumonia, septicaemia and organ failure, with about a 30 per cent fatality rate. In the US Army, a total of 43,000 servicemen died of the illness in Europe.

GLOBAL KILLER

The disease – often known historically as 'Spanish flu' despite the fact that the disease was probably imported from the United States, not Spain – was startlingly contagious, and soon spread from military to civilian communities around the world. More than 400,000 German civilians died during 1918 alone, and it ➤➤

KEY FACTS

Disease begins on the battlefields of France in the spring of 1918.

More than 70 million people die of the influenza over the next two years.

Disease appears to be most lethal against those aged from 20 to 40 years.

Highest death toll in India – 16 million fatalities.

During the influenza pandemic, emergency treatment and isolation centres were set up throughout Europe and the United States. A basic understanding of disease transmission prevented the disease becoming a second Black Death in the West.

Above: The influenza pandemic originated in the insanitary conditions of the Western Front at the end of World War I. A general state of poor health among many of the war-weary soldiers would have suppressed immune systems and facilitated the spread of the disease.

reached the United Kingdom in May, killing 230,000 people by the beginning of winter. A total of 675,000 Americans would die of the influenza, despite the fact that the country was well developed with a modern health system.

SOCIAL EMERGENCY

In the developing world, the effects were even worse – 16 million people died in India. Unusually, those most likely to die from the disease were individuals in the 20–40 age range, rather than children or old people. Its virulence was also extraordinary – many people went from being perfectly healthy to being dead within 24 hours, suffocated by their pneumonic lungs.

The international emergency completely overloaded medical resources and mortuaries. In the United States, special flu ordinances included restrictions on travel, the distribution of gauze face masks, the banning of sales in department stores and even time limits placed on the length of funeral gatherings (only 15 minutes). The pandemic subsided towards the end of 1919, but today scientists are aware of the potential for new strains of influenza to have equally devastating effects. ∎

A court conducts its proceedings outdoors as part of a wave of measures to prevent the spread of the influenza virus. The death toll from the pandemic was greatest in the developing world, where poverty and close-packed housing ensured a rapid infection rate.

TORNADO

THE PEOPLE OF THE AMERICAN MIDWEST HAVE ENDURED TORNADOES FOR CENTURIES, BUT FEW HAVE HAD SUCH DESTRUCTIVE EFFECTS AS THAT EXPERIENCED ON 18 MARCH 1925.

Around the town of Ellington, Missouri, the day began with extremely mild temperatures of 15°C (60°F), which had risen towards 21°C (70°F) by around lunchtime. However, the presence of a cold front to the southwest and the ingress of moist air from the Gulf of Mexico was creating the perfect breeding grounds for a tornado. At around 1 p.m., the skies darkened into a storm system northwest of Ellington, which in turn produced a tornado of immense destructive force.

F5 TORNADO

Historical records place the 1925 tornado in the F5 category of strength – the most powerful classification of tornado. At its height, it was about 1.6km (1 mile) wide and had internal wind speeds of 482km/h (300mph), enough to blast down any structure in its path. For three-and-a-half hours, the tornado carved itself across three states – Missouri, Illinois and Indiana – taking in ➤➤

KEY FACTS

- **18 March 1925** – a tornado touches down at 1.01 p.m. near Ellington, Missouri, and dissipates at 4.30 p.m. near Petersburg, Indiana.
- **A total** of 695 people are killed and 2027 injured.
- **The tornado** has an average cross-land speed of 100km/h (63mph) and internal wind speeds of up to 482km/h (300mph).

The internal wind speeds of the 1925 tornado reached an estimated 482km/h (300mph), and not only turned houses into matchwood (or onto their sides, as here), but also created lethal missiles from the debris.

13 counties and wrecking more than 19 communities. Its first victim was a farmer near Ellington, and it then tracked northeast through the towns and farming communities of Missouri, killing 11 people.

CONTINUED DESTRUCTION

Far worse was to come in Illinois. Thirty-four people were killed in the town of Gorham, and equal or greater destruction was wrought on De Soto, Hurst-Bush, Zeigler, West Frankfort, Eighteen, Parrish, Crossville and Murphysboro (which suffered 234 dead, the biggest individual community death toll). During the 40 minutes the tornado spent in Illinois, more than 600 people died and nearly 1500 were injured. Entire towns were wiped off the face of the earth. Yet even now the energy of the tornado had not abated, and it crossed into Indiana. More than 70 people, mainly in rural areas, were killed and much of the town of Princeton destroyed. Thankfully, the destruction was nearing its end and, after 352km (219 miles) of travel, the tornado finally dissipated 5km (3 miles) southwest of Petersburg, Indiana. It had killed 695 people, injured over 2000 and created property damage totalling $16.5 million. Over 15,000 homes had been destroyed, and the event remains the United States' worst tornado disaster. ■

Above: The clean-up following the tornado lasted for several months, and the total damage cost reached nearly $17 million. The disaster prompted the US government to initiate programmes for the development of better tornado warning systems.

Half of the population of Murphysboro was rendered homeless by the tornado. In total, the town lost around 1200 homes as the tornado cut a path 1.6km (1 mile) wide and 3km (2 miles) long through the community.

R101 AIRSHIP

THE R101 WAS MEANT TO BE A FLAGSHIP OF BRITISH AVIATION.

It was built under the auspices of the British Air Ministry, with production beginning in 1926 at the Royal Airship Works in Cardington, Bedfordshire. From its very first days, it was dogged by problems and concerns. Plans to fit the airship with engines which used hydrogen power failed in the design stage, and the R101 was instead fitted with far heavier diesel-powered engines. In turn, this dramatically reduced its intended lifting capacity from 54 tons (60 tonnes) to 32 tons (35 tonnes).

DESIGN PROBLEMS

Such issues were compounded by far more serious problems in the airship's flight performance. Initial flight trials showed the R101 had an acute tendency to lose altitude. Indeed, at the 1930 Hendon air show, a precipitous loss of height saw the R101 nearly crash into the ground. The problem may have come from a combination of faulty controls and gas-valve leaks, but was not fundamentally resolved. Instead, engineers simply increased the gas capacity of the airship, and the craft obtained its flight permit. ➤➤

KEY FACTS

1926 – production begins on the R101, with serious flight problems emerging over the next four years.

4 October 1930 – the R101 sets out on the first leg of a voyage to Karachi, India.

The R101 crashes in France near Beauvois, catches fire and explodes, killing 46 passengers at the crash site.

The wreckage of the R101 suggests the intensity of the fire that destroyed it. As the R101 crashed, the starboard engine car was twisted around, and the hot engine ignited gas flowing out from the ripped forward gas bags.

Above: The R101, despite its short, tragic history, was a beautiful craft. It was part of Britain's attempt to catch up with and exceed German advances in airship technology, although the practicality of airships for both military and civilian use was questionable.

On 4 October 1930, the R101 took off from Cardington on an intended voyage to Karachi, India. Despite its problems, the ship looked magnificent. It stretched to 237m (777ft) long, had two decks and a 60-cover dining room, and had a total capacity of 1.7 million cubic metres (5.5 million cubic feet). Aboard the airship were several important British dignitaries, including Lord Christopher Thomson, Secretary of State for Air, and Sir Sefton Brancker, Director of Civil Aviation.

CRASH LANDING

Under the command of Lieutenant Carmichael Irwin, the airship was moving near Beauvois, north of Paris, when its instability problems struck again. Strong winds picked up and the R101 began a sudden drop in altitude (survivors of the crash report that the forward gas bags had been ripped open in the wind). Irwin was unable to arrest its decline, and the airship crash-landed, relatively smoothly, into a hillside. However, the escaping hydrogen gas ignited on a hot engine, causing a fire and subsequent violent explosions. Only eight people of the R101's 54 passengers managed to escape, and two of those died later in hospital. It brought to an end British experiments with airship passenger flight. ■

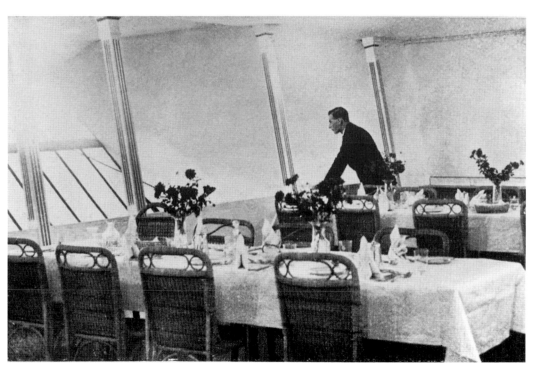

The R101 was set to impress the world, this shows the lavish main dining room on board which had a capacity of 1.7 million cubic metres (5.5 million cubic feet). Important British dignitaries were set to dine here.

CHINA FLOODING

THE YELLOW RIVER IN CHINA IS FAR AND AWAY THE WORLD'S MOST DANGEROUS WATERCOURSE.

In the past 2000 years of recorded history, the river has produced massive flooding on more than 1000 separate occasions, with some huge death tolls – the flood of 1887, for example, killed more than two million people.

BURST BANKS

The primary reasons for the aquatic unpredictability of the river are its size and composition. At around 4800km (3000 miles) long, the Yellow River begins in the mountains of northern Qinhai province and terminates on the coast of the Yellow Sea. Such an immense waterway is rendered unstable by the river's extremely high silt content. Running in parts at 60 per cent by volume, the silt concentrations are constantly reshaping the contours of the Yellow River. Also, and more seriously, these can create blockages, which result in burst banks. Water engineers have struggled against this problem since the third century, but even today the river continues to thwart the best efforts. (The name 'Yellow River' ➤➤

KEY FACTS

Huang He (Yellow River) and Yangtze River flood between July and November 1931, inundating more than 155,000 square kilometres (60,000 square miles) of land.

140,000 people drown in the floodwaters.

Over three million people die as a result of subsequent disease and famine.

Photographers were present to document the terrible effects of the Chinese flooding and subsequent famine. Such images had a powerful effect abroad, particularly in the United States, which maintained a large missionary presence in China.

Above: The flood of 1931 affected the unfortunate Chinese population in three ways – drowning, disease and famine. The last two enhanced the effects of each other, famine killing thousands of people and the corpses encouraging disease.

derives from the colour of the silt, the Chinese title for the river being the Huang He.)

MONTHS OF RAIN

In 1931, the Yellow River unleashed a disaster of almost biblical proportions. In July, following a long period of drought in the region, vast rainstorms over central China brought the Yellow River's waters up and over the banks. The rains continued until November, flooding 108,000 square kilometres (42,000 square miles) of land, washing away crops and inundating hundreds of towns, villages and cities. At one point, a water station on the river was measuring an output of 15,800cu m/s (557,898cu ft/s). The middle and lower reaches of the Yangtze (which is connected to the Yellow River) were also breached, flooding 3.3 million hectares (7.9 million acres) of land. Up to 140,000 people were killed by actual flood waters, mostly as a result of dykes and dams suddenly breaking, but the true horror of the flood came from the resulting famine, plus the spread of waterborne diseases, which was accelerated by the presence of around two million decaying livestock floating in the flood waters. The final death toll numbered around 3.7 million people, making it one of the costliest natural disasters in human history. ■

The huge extent of the 1931 flooding meant that day-to-day life was often conducted in waist-deep water.

THE HINDENBURG DISASTER

THE DESTRUCTION OF THE *HINDENBURG* AT LAKEHURST NAVAL
AIR STATION, NEW JERSEY, IN 1937 HAS GONE DOWN IN HISTORY
PRIMARILY BECAUSE OF THE STRIKING FILM FOOTAGE CAPTURED.

The *Hindenburg* was built by Luftschiffbau Zeppelin in 1935 to
extend the success the company had experienced with its earlier
luxury passenger airship, the *Graf Zeppelin*. The *Hindenburg* was a
truly inspiring craft. It was 245m (804ft) long and 41m (135ft) in
diameter, with a transatlantic carrying capacity of 50 passengers
and 61 crew. By the end of 1936 the airship was making regular
trips from its native Germany to Rio de Janeiro and New York,
carrying over 2600 passengers in that year alone.

LETHAL CONTENTS

Unlike airships found in the United States and many other
European countries, the *Hindenburg* gained its lift through the
flammable hydrogen gas, rather than the non-flammable helium.
(Hydrogen was used because of a US military embargo on helium.) The *Hindenberg* contained
200,000m^3 (7,060,000ft^3) of hydrogen, but the airship's engineers were confident that it was safely
contained within its huge gas bag (there was even a smoking room on board). The airship featured a ➤➤

The Hindenburg *was, in 1937, an emblem of Nazi power and was frequently used in German propaganda events.*

➤➤

Above: The total destruction of the Hindenburg *brought the airship age to an end. The refinement of fixed-wing aircraft technology made the airship obsolete for both passenger transportation and military usage, and remaining German airships were simply stripped down for aviation parts and metals.*

special coating to prevent sparks and it used non-conductive structures around its aluminium frame.

TERMINAL DESTINATION

On 3 May 1937 the *Hindenburg* took off from Frankfurt with 97 people on board, its destination New York. The trip usually took two to three days, and on 6 May the airship was already over the eastern coastline of the States. The landing at Lakehurst Naval Air Station was delayed owing to bad weather, so the captain, Commander Max Pruss, treated the passengers to a lingering flight over New York City. Finally, at 6.12 p.m., Pruss received the authorization to dock. At 7.25 p.m. the *Hindenburg* finally approached its mooring mast at about 82m (270ft) above ground. Suddenly flames were spotted at the rear of the airship, then the whole craft erupted in a massive fireball. The entire craft was reduced to a charred skeleton in only 37 seconds, the event captured on film and accompanied by the frenzied reportage of radio reporter Herbert Morrison. Incredibly, 62 people managed to escape by jumping from the passenger compartments and running to safety. The rest were burned to death. The actual cause of the ignition is still not known, the explanations range from a bomb to a spark generated by build-up of static electricity. ■

The Hindenburg *crashes to the ground in flames, with the mooring station clearly visible in the foreground. It is possible that the airship's wet mooring lines created static sparks along the* Hindenburg's *aluminium frame when they touched the station.*

NANKING

The now infamous 'rape of Nanking' took place during the second Sino-Japanese War (1937–45), although the context of armed struggle does not adequately explain the horror of what occurred in the city.

The war began on 7 July 1937 with a Japanese invasion of northern and western China, and the troops soon advanced southwards. Shanghai fell to the Japanese in mid-August, after which the Japanese X Corps began a westward advance towards the capital of nationalist China, Nanking.

BLOODBATH

By 1 December, when the Japanese launched their offensive against Nanking, the city's already large population had been swollen by the arrival of up to 700,000 war refugees. The nationalist government of Chiang Kai Shek had abandoned Nanking for Chungking in Szechwan province, and from 10 December Japanese forces began closing the jaws of a pincer movement around the city. Nanking fell to the Japanese forces on 15 December 1937. ➤➤

KEY FACTS

- **1 December 1937** – Japanese launch an offensive against Nanking, the city falling on 15 December.
- **Japanese forces** systematically murder an estimated 200,000 people within Nanking over a period of six weeks.
- **February 1938** – the violence stops owing to the spread of disease and a worldwide outcry.

Japan had been in an ongoing state of war with China since the early 1930s. Japanese militarism meant that many field armies in China acted with an authority almost independent of the government back in Tokyo.

Above: Although China had a large army, it was no match for advanced Japanese combined-arms operations. By the end of 1937, most of western China was in Japanese hands.

What occurred next defies explanation. With tacit, or often explicit, approval from their officers, the Japanese troops embarked on six weeks of unrestrained murder, torture and rape against Nanking's population.

A KILLING SPREE

At first, the atrocities began with a wholesale massacre of prisoners of war, thousands being machine-gunned along the banks of the Yangtze. However, it did not stop there. Around 80,000 women were gang raped, most being killed afterwards, suffering horrific sexual mutilations. Japanese units organized beheading competitions, stacking up hundreds of heads along walls. Children were bayoneted and tortured without mercy, and it seemed that the Japanese troops were constantly on the search for new ways to put people to death. Many killings were photographed and made into postcards, which were then sent home to families – the dehumanization of the Chinese seemed to extend for the Japanese civilian population. The final death toll of the rape of Nanking was around 200,000 people, and it seems that only the spread of cholera and typhus in February 1938, and the outcry from Western Europe, put a brake on the massacre. ∎

Japanese units behaved terribly in victory. Some organized speed beheading competitions on the streets of Nanking.

SIEGE OF LENINGRAD

THE SIEGE OF LENINGRAD WAS NOT ONLY AN EPIC AND DREADFUL CHAPTER IN THE HISTORY OF WORLD WAR II, BUT A PROFOUND HUMAN DISASTER THAT COST THE LIVES OF AN ESTIMATED ONE MILLION PEOPLE AS WELL.

In June 1941, Germany invaded the Soviet Union in Operation Barbarossa. Its advance into the Soviet heartlands was separated into three enormous thrusts, one southwards towards the Ukraine, one directly east towards Moscow, and the third hooking northwards towards the city of Leningrad, Russia's second city.

THE GERMAN ADVANCE

In those first months of Barbarossa, the German advance seemed inexorable. By 15 September, the German Army Group North had wrapped itself almost completely around Leningrad, save for a tenuous rail link from Tikhvin, which snaked up to Lake Ladoga to the north of the city. Trapped inside Leningrad were 2.6 million people. The Germans were unable to take the city itself, but on 9 November they cut the rail link at Tikhvin. Even before Tikhvin fell, the Leningrad population had only four to eight weeks of ➤

> ### KEY FACTS
>
> - **22 June 1944** – German invasion of the Soviet Union, Operation Barbarossa, commences.
> - **15 September** – Leningrad is put under blockade by the Germans, and food reserves in Leningrad effectively run out in two months.
> - **The siege** is maintained for 900 days, during which time around 950,000 people die as a result of starvation, disease or enemy action.

Leningrad was kept under a persistent artillery fire for almost the entire length of the siege. The Luftwaffe also added to the misery of Leningrad's people, the bombing raids curtailed only by the Germans' eventual loss of air superiority.

Above: Soviet forces would ultimately exact a terrible revenge on the German soldiers and people for the destruction of their homeland. At least one million German prisoners of war were starved and worked to death in Soviet camps following World War II.

food, and as one of the cruellest winters on record set in, the population simply began to starve. (Tikhvin was later recaptured, although with marginal impact on food supplies.)

MEALS OF PAPER AND GLUE

Around 30 tons (33 tonnes) of supplies passed across ice roads on the frozen Lake Ladoga during the winter, and via boats during the summer, but this lifeline was grossly inadequate to feed a population of nearly three million. Everything consumable was eaten, including horses, dogs, cats, crows and rats; when even these food sources were exhausted, glue, candles, paper and leather became foodstuffs. On 25 December 1941, more than 3500 people died in a single day. Furthermore, the population had to contend with constant artillery and air bombardments from the Germans – more than 150,000 shells were fired into the city during the siege. Soviet forces broke the siege of Leningrad in February 1944, by which time around 950,000 people had starved or frozen to death, or been killed by enemy action. It was just one of the many tragic episodes of the 1941–45 German-Soviet war, during which the Soviet Union lost an estimated 25 million soldiers and civilians. ■

Although Leningrad ultimately survived the German siege, the urban landscape was utterly wrecked by the war.

HARTFORD CIRCUS FIRE

AT THE HEIGHT OF WORLD WAR II, A VISITING CIRCUS WAS ALWAYS A WELCOME DISTRACTION FOR THE COMMUNITIES OF THE UNITED STATES.

The arrival of the Ringling Bros and Barnum & Bailey circus in Hartford, Connecticut, in July 1944 was no exception. On the afternoon of 6 July 1944, the circus was in full swing and the large circus tent was packed with 7000 spectators, a large percentage of them being children (the afternoon performance meant that many adults were in work, especially as wartime industrialization utilized women as well as men).

INCENDIARY TENT

During the performance, a fire broke out in one corner of the tent, and quickly spread across the canvas and wood structure. The animals were quickly ushered from the tent, as the crowd descended into panic, with people stampeding towards the exit in their haste to escape. Unfortunately this was actually near the epicentre of the fire, and was also partially blocked by steel railings. Speed was of the essence, as the fire was racing across ➤➤

KEY FACTS

- **6 July 1944** – fire breaks out in the Ringling Bros and Barnum & Bailey circus in Hartford, Connecticut.
- **The highly** flammable canvas waterproofing results in the complete destruction of the circus tent in a matter of only six minutes.
- **The final** death toll comes to 168, with more than 50 per cent of the casualties being children.

Circus-goers flee for their lives. The whole Barnum & Bailey circus tent was destroyed in just six minutes.

Above: J.A. Bailey of the Barnum & Bailey circus. Bailey and his partner responded creditably to the disaster.

the circus roof (the canvas had been waterproofed with paraffin and petrol). A terrible fact revealed after the fire was that the circus owners had previously attempted to purchase a special type of canvas fire-proofing developed by the US military, but were turned down because the military refused its use by civilians. In only three minutes, the whole tent was ablaze and the roof collapsed inwards, and in just six minutes the entire tent had been reduced to ash.

CORPORATE RESPONSIBILITY

In addition to the many hundreds of seriously injured, the fire resulted in 168 deaths, of whom 68 were children under the age of 15. The fire sent ripples throughout the United States – in a country which did not directly suffer from any significant homeland war damage, the fire stood out as an appalling tragedy. Five members of the circus management served custodial sentences for manslaughter, and the circus spent the next 10 years settling the millions of dollars of claims against it. To its lasting credit, it did not contest the claims and even aided the judicial process in its smooth handling of cases. ■

Crowds gather around the site of the circus fire disaster. In addition to the dead, a total of 487 people were injured. The site where the fire took place was later turned into a housing project.

WILHELM GUSTLOFF

THE WORLD'S WORST MARITIME DISASTER WAS TO TAKE PLACE ON 30 JANUARY 1945.

In terms of sheer loss of life, the sinking of the *Wilhelm Gustloff* far overshadows any other single-vessel disaster, the combined death tolls of both the *Titanic* and the *Lusitania* coming to only a quarter of the number of those who died in the Baltic that day.

SUBMARINE ATTACK

The *Wilhelm Gustloff* had been launched in 1937 and initially served as a prestige cruise liner for the German *Kraft durch Freude* (Strength through Joy) movement. With the onset of war in 1939, however, the vessel took on a number of different roles, including hospital ship, before being anchored at Gotenhafen on the Baltic

Sea from November 1940 as a barracks ship for the Kreigsmarine. There she remained until January 1945, by which time Germany had descended into apocalyptic chaos. On the eastern front, Russian forces had already penetrated into the Reich territory of East Prussia, and millions of East Prussians now began an exodus to the West with the hope of naval evacuation from the Baltic. This exodus in itself was an awesome disaster – an estimated one million exposed Prussians died in the subzero conditions of that terrible winter, while those who stayed behind faced rape and murder by the Soviet troops. ➤➤

KEY FACTS

30 January 1945 – The *Wilhelm Gustloff* sets sail from Gotenhafen with 10,582 refugees, crew and military personnel on board.

9.30 p.m. – the Russian submarine *S-13* hits the ship with three torpedoes

The *Wilhelm Gustloff* sinks in 50 minutes, and 9343 people die in the disaster.

The Wilhelm Gustloff *had a previously happy existence as a cruise ship for the National Socialist tourist industry, taking German citizens on cruises to destinations ranging from Italy to Norway.*

The *Wilhelm Gustloff* was pressed into service again to assist with evacuations. On the night of 30 January 1945, she left port. Chronically overcrowded with 10,582 refugees on board, she launched into conditions of high winds, poor visibility (it was snowing) and freezing sea and air temperatures. She had no military escort. At 9.08 p.m., the *Wilhelm Gustloff* was torpedoed by Russian submarine *S-13*, which had been waiting off the Baltic coast.

MARITIME CATASTROPHE

The great liner was hit by three torpedoes along the length of the hull, and began a catastrophic slide under the water. Amid scenes of unimaginable horror, thousands of men, women and children went down with the ship or 'escaped' into the waters, where they died within minutes from hypothermia or drowning. A total of 9343 people lost their lives in this single incident, the remainder being rescued by a collection of small German ships that raced to the scene. Terribly, two other large refugees ships – the *General Steuben* and *Goya* – would also be sunk during the refugee operations, at a loss of a further 10,000 lives. ∎

Above: The Wilhelm Gustloff *sets out on a safer voyage earlier in its history. The Russian submarine captain responsible for the 1945 torpedo attack was later sentenced to three years' hard labour by the Soviets for drunken behaviour, and not until 1960 were his claims to have sunk the* Wilhelm Gustloff *finally accepted.*

Hitler and various other Nazi dignitaries inspect the Wilhelm Gustloff. *It was Hitler's insistence to fight to the very end that made the evacuation of East Prussia a terrible necessity, the population rightly fearing Soviet retribution.*

MODERN DISASTERS 1945 – PRESENT DAY

The world has seen more technological revolution since 1945 than it witnessed in all the preceding centuries put together. While much of this technology, particularly in areas of computerization and transport, has immeasurably improved life, it has also provided the ingredients for hi-tech disaster. Space exploration remains a dangerous pursuit, illustrated by the loss of two space shuttles and numerous other space vehicles in airborne or launch-pad accidents. The Tenerife air crash (1977), the Bhopal gas disaster (1984) and the Chernobyl explosion (1986) are further examples of how human beings often cannot control what they create.

Left: The September 11 attacks on the United States are one of the most important world events of the twenty-first century.

CHINA FAMINE

THE APPALLING FACT ABOUT THE CHINESE FAMINE OF 1958–61 IS THAT IT WAS ALMOST ENTIRELY BROUGHT ABOUT BY HUMAN INTERFERENCE IN AGRICULTURAL PROCESSES.

In 1958, the communist party of Mao Tse Tung had been in power for 10 years, and was actively engaged in a vast project of social and economic engineering.

MANMADE CATASTROPHE

China was at this time primarily an agricultural nation, and one of the government's principal objectives was to rationalize agricultural production along Communist lines. It based its policies upon those enacted in the Soviet Union, with a particular focus upon the theories of Trofim Denisovitch Lysenko, one of Stalin's foremost agricultural scientists. Unfortunately, Lysenko had little understanding of science, and his policies resulted in a famine that killed millions.

Undeterred, Mao Tse Tung forged ahead with a dreadful series of 'reforms', which included the order that farmers increase the number of seeds planted per acre from a typical 1.5 million ➤➤

KEY FACTS

1958 – the Communist government of Mao Tse Tung implements a series of disastrous agricultural reforms.

The reforms result in huge crop failure and resulting famine.

Estimated final death toll for between 1958 and 1961 is 40 million.

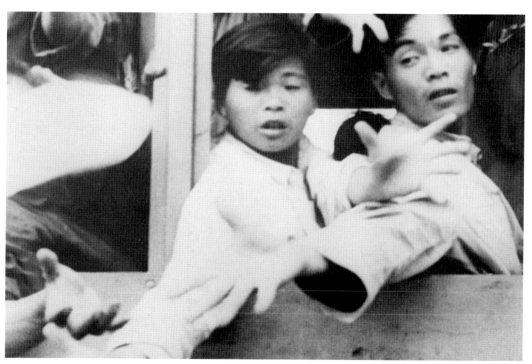

Despite the fact that millions of people were starving to death throughout China, no one was allowed to acknowledge publicly that there was a problem. Those that did faced imprisonment and execution.

➼

Above: Trofim Denisovitch Lysenko developed some of the most disastrous agricultural theories in history, responsible for millions of deaths.

seedlings per hectare (2.5 acres) before the reforms, to an astonishing 12–15 million seedlings in the same area by 1959. The result was that the seeds were too closely packed to grow. Other measures included an attempt to exterminate the bird population (resulting in destructive levels of insect activity) and a prohibition against the use of fertilizers.

POLITICAL TERROR

The result of these so-called improvements to agricultural policy was an absolutely catastrophic crop failure, and a devastating famine swept the entire nation. Those who highlighted deficiencies in the Communist policy were quickly arrested and disappeared. In fact, Mao Tse Tung even insisted that the famine was the result of political subversion, and executed thousands of starving people for 'hiding' rice supplies. Although no conclusive data is available from the period, it is now estimated that between 30 and 40 million people died during the great famine. The famine ranks as one of the great political crimes of all the history, and stands as a condemnation of Communist China's early policies. ■

Chinese citizens finally get a full meal after years of famine. Despite China's disastrous attempts at an agricultural revolution, countries such as Cambodia, Ethiopia and North Korea attempted similar ventures and created their own famines.

BAIKONUR EXPLOSION

**IN 1960, THE SPACE RACE BETWEEN THE UNITED STATES AND
THE SOVIET UNION WAS HOTTING UP.**

The development of advanced rocketry was not only about space
exploration, but also concerned with delivery systems for atomic
warheads, so the pressure was on in both the East and the West
to produce new, more capable vehicles.

RUSHED PROJECT

In 1960, the Soviets had heavy expectations for their R-16 ICBM,
a missile 31m (101ft) long, weighing 141 tons (155 tonnes) and
capable of flying to targets 13,000km (8078 miles) away. Testing
of the rocket began on 26 September, with Mitrofan Nedelin,
Marshall of Artillery, and Mikhail Yangel, chief designer, with both
men eager to demonstrate the new rocket to Soviet officialdom.
A launch date of 23 October was set. The R-16 was installed on
its launch pad at the Baikonur Space Centre on 21 October, and
was fully fuelled two days later. Now everyone was waiting for the
actual launch. Critically, in the hours before the launch, some
150 people, including Yangel and Nedelin, milled around the ➤➤

KEY FACTS

21 October 1960 – the R-16
rocket is readied for launch
at Baikonur Space Centre
in Kazakhstan.

Following a one-day delay, the
R-16 is scheduled for launch
on 24 October.

The R-16 explodes on the
launch pad prior to launch,
killing 92 people and
wounding 47.

Continuing troubles ... inspectors view the damage to building no. 112 after a roof collapse at the Baikonur Space Centre in 2002.

➤➤

launch pad, despite prohibitions being in place for safety reason. During this time, engineers discovered a fuel leak in the rocket, but because draining off the fuel to make a repair would have meant scrapping the launch entirely, the leak was merely kept 'under control'. Several other problems occurred, and the launch was put back to the next day.

CUTTING CORNERS

On the 24th, everyone was under extreme technical, and political, pressure to make a launch. Then, at 6.45 p.m., only 30 minutes before the launch time and with 250 people around the launch pad trying to sort out ominous electrical problems, the rocket's second-stage engine suddenly ignited from a leaky fuel valve, detonating the first-stage fuel tank below it in a ball of flame 120m (384ft) across. A total of 92 people were burnt to death on or around the launch pad, with others attempting to flee to safety with their clothes and hair on fire. Some bodies were never recovered – they had been reduced to ash by the heat of the rocket fuel. Forty-nine others were seriously injured. Nedelin was among the dead, paying the ultimate price for succumbing to political pressure and ignoring the need for technical safety. ■

Above: The Baikonur Space Centre remains in use today. Here a Soyuz craft carrying the Beagle 2 *Mars lander is launched in June 2003.*

A large funeral procession for Mitrofan Nedelin, who died in the space-centre explosion, winds around the Baikonur base.

ABERFAN DISASTER

THE ABERFAN DISASTER OF 21 OCTOBER 1966, STILL CASTS A SHADOW OVER THE PEOPLE OF SOUTH WALES, UNITED KINGDOM, AND IS ONE OF THE WORST ACCIDENTS IN BRITISH HISTORY.

Aberfan is a small village in Wales near the town of Merthyr Tydfil. In the 1960s, the South Wales region was dominated by the coal-mining industry, and Aberfan sat in the shadow of a mountain on which were tipped huge deposits of mine waste.

LANDSLIDE

On the early morning of 21 October 1966, the village went about its normal business, and some 250 pupils were in attendance at the Pantglas Junior School, set about 182m (600ft) below the summit of the mountain. They attended assembly, sang the hymn 'All Things Bright and Beautiful', then went to their regular classes. The children of the school were used to the sounds of coal-mining activity, particularly of waste tipping, but at 9.15 a.m. they heard a louder, thunderous noise approaching their school. Unbeknown to them, one of the coal waste tips above them – some 500,000 tons (551,155 tonnes) of black slurry – was sweeping down the ➤➤

KEY FACTS

1966 – Spring water and heavy rain destabilize a coal slag heap above the village.

October 21 – Half a million tons (551,155 tonnes) of slurry slide downwards, burying a junior school and 20 houses.

144 people are killed, including 116 schoolchildren.

Pantglas Junior School was almost entirely submerged under metres of filthy coal slurry. Rescue work was hampered by dangers such as fractured gas mains and weakened building structures.

Above: A survivor of Pantglas School later recounted: 'The sound got louder and nearer, until I could see the black out of the window. I can't remember any more, but I woke up to find that a horrible nightmare had just begun'.

mountain in a wave 12m (40ft) high. The torrent of waste engulfed the school, demolishing the walls and filling up the classrooms, and also submerging 20 houses in the village. Eyewitnesses report a terrible silence descending over the village in the immediate aftermath of the landslide. The emergency services went into action, as did hundreds of local people who rushed to the site with shovels, ready to help. In such a small, close-knit mining community, almost everybody had relatives or children implicated in the disaster.

TRAUMATIC TASK

It would take a week of digging to uncover all the bodies. In Pantglas School, a total of 116 schoolchildren – most aged from 7–10 years – were killed, along with five of their teachers, and the final death toll in the village was 144. An official inquiry into the disaster found that locals had warned the National Coal Board (NCB) of an underground spring beneath one of the main slag heaps, but their warnings were ignored. The spring water, combined with two days of rain, had loosened the tip and caused it to slide. Half a century on, the village still lives with the scars of that awful morning. ■

The huge numbers of people travelling in vehicles to Aberfan to help with the rescue effort actually blocked up the approach roads, and had to be cleared to allow rescue services vehicles through.

BANGLADESH CYCLONE

BANGLADESH HAS HAD A LONG HISTORY OF SUFFERING UNDER THE EFFECTS OF EXTREME WEATHER.

Between 1970 and 1998 alone, the country experienced some 170 natural disasters, ranging from severe flooding to prolonged drought, all of which have cost millions of lives.

VULNERABLE REGION

Tropical cyclones are an unwelcome perennial visitor to Bangladesh, occurring each year from April to May and from September to November (4 per cent of the entire total of the world's cyclones strike Bangladesh). Tremendous flooding often occurs during these events, as Bangladesh is a low-lying, mostly flat country, which opens out into the waters of the Bay of Bengal, while major river systems such as the Ganges, Brahmaputra, Padma and Jamuna run out to the sea through Bangladesh from the mountains of India. On 12–13 November 1970, the country was hit by a tropical cyclone of truly awesome destructive potential. The weather system brought in winds of 200km/h (124mph) and driving rain. The winds in themselves caused huge damage, tearing down the ➤➤

KEY FACTS

12–13 November 1970 – a powerful cyclone with wind speeds of more than 200km/h (124mph) strikes Bangladesh.

Between 300,000 and 500,000 people are killed in a matter of hours when the storm generates a 7m (23ft) surge from the waters of the Bay of Bengal, which inundates thousands of kilometres of territory.

The inundation in Bangladesh in 1970 trapped thousands of people on high land or in those buildings that had not been destroyed by the immensely powerful cyclonic winds.

Above: A vaccination programme to guard against waterborne diseases such as cholera and typhus became an immediate priority in the aftermath of the cyclone disaster. The flooding resulted in the mixing of sewerage and drinking water systems.

vulnerable housing (as most of the inhabited areas of Bangladesh are in the delta of the Brahmaputra and Ganges, houses are frequently constructed on platforms or high embankments to escape floodwaters).

STORM SURGE

The most damaging force was to come from the sea. A storm surge – a rise in the sea level caused by storm-force winds – drove a 7m (23ft) wall of water inland, inundating the flatlands, wiping out crops, livestock and people, and wrecking housing.

The final death toll of that one dreadful night in Bangladesh is estimated at around 500,000, with some estimates of the final death toll, including the aftereffects of disease and starvation, climbing closer to one million. Hundreds of thousands of people were also left homeless. Since the 1970 disaster, Bangladesh has made some efforts towards providing storm shelters for its population, although the country regularly suffers disasters. In 1991, for example, another wrecking cyclone killed 138,000 people in this long-suffering country. ∎

The typical housing of Bangladesh was poorly equipped to deal with the power of the cyclone. As seen here, many of the houses consisted of little more than a wooden framework roofed with mats of vegetation.

TENERIFE AIR CRASH

THE WORLD'S WORST AIRCRAFT-COLLISION DISASTER OCCURRED ON 28 MARCH 1977 ON THE SMALL ISLAND OF TENERIFE, ONE OF THE SPANISH-CONTROLLED CANARY ISLANDS FOUND OFF THE COAST OF NORTH AFRICA.

Tenerife's main airport, Los Rodeos, was normally a fairly sedate destination, coping with little more than a steady intake of tourist flights. However, on 28 March air traffic was heavily increased by planes being diverted away from Las Palmas airport on Gran Canaria (another of the Canary Islands) after a bomb incident. Early in the afternoon, two Boeing 747s landed, one a Pan-American flight from New York and the other a KLM (Royal Dutch Airlines) flight from Amsterdam.

COMMUICATIONS FAILURE
The two flights parked in Los Rodeos for around three hours. During this time, the weather worsened over the airport, with thick fog and heavy rain reducing visibility to just a few hundred metres. However, by five o'clock Las Palmas was once again receiving flights. Because of the congestion at Los Rodeos, the ➤

The sheer scale of the devastation caused by the Tenerife air crash is strikingly apparent here. After the initial impact, the KLM jet managed to climb to an altitude of about 30m (100ft) before losing control and dropping back to earth in a fireball.

➼

Above: The landing gear of one of the Boeings lies on the runway at Tenerife. The massive impact of the two aircraft colliding resulted in the total destruction of both planes.

captains of the two Boeings (Captain Victor Grubbs on the Pan Am aircraft, Captain Jacob Van Zanten for KLM) were instructed to taxi down the runway itself and turn 180 degrees at the end for take-off, the KLM flight going first. Grubbs followed the Dutch aircraft down the runway at a distance – the Pan Am aircraft was meant to move out the way when both had taxied down to take-off position.

RUNWAY COLLISION

At 5.06 p.m., the KLM aircraft was in its take-off position, with Grubbs' Boeing still taxiing up the runway. For reasons which still remain unclear, Van Kanten decided to go ahead with take-off. Grubbs immediately radioed out that he was still on the runway, but the message was lost in static noise. Grubbs attempted to swing his aircraft off the runway, but it was too late. At take-off speed, the KLM Boeing slammed into the side of the Pan Am aircraft. Both aircraft erupted in enormous fires, with the KLM jet lifting off briefly before crashing. Although 61 people from the Pan Am flight survived, a total of 583 people died in the accident. ∎

There were no survivors at all from the KLM flight, which was utterly destroyed when it hit the ground approximately 250m (820ft) from the initial point of impact with the Pan Am aircraft.

SAMASTIPUR TRAIN DISASTER

INDIA HAS ONE OF THE BIGGEST AND BUSIEST RAIL NETWORKS IN THE WORLD, SECOND ONLY TO THOSE OF RUSSIA AND CHINA, ALTHOUGH IT EXCEEDS EVEN THOSE COUNTRIES IN TERMS OF THE DISTANCE TRAVELLED BY ITS PASSENGERS.

There are 63,000km (39,147 miles) of rail track and chronic overcrowding on the trains, which carry around 11 million passengers every year, so it is inevitable that India is visited by train disasters every few years. Some of these can be appalling in their magnitude.

OVERCROWDED TRAIN

Arguably the world's worst train disaster occurred on 6 June 1981 in Bahir. On that date, a regular passenger service train was near the town of Samastipur. Post-accident evidence suggests that the train was typically overcrowded, the numbers of fee-paying passengers being swelled dramatically by possibly hundreds of people travelling without tickets, many of them hanging on to the outside of the train. Details concerning what happened next are unclear, but what is certain is that the train derailed while crossing ➤➤

KEY FACTS

6 June 1981 – the locomotive and seven carriages of a passenger train plummet over a bridge near Samastipur in Bihar, India.

The train falls into the Bagmati River, where up to 1000 people are drowned or killed in the impact.

The exact cause of the rail disaster is never fully determined.

People gather around the wreckage of the train crash at Samastipur. The death toll of the crash was worsened by the large numbers of people travelling on the train illegally, India's extreme cases of poverty making tickets an unaffordable luxury for many.

a bridge over the river Bagmati, taking seven passenger carriages over the side of the bridge and plummeting into the river below. The final death toll of the accident is hard to ascertain. The number of bodies recovered came to 212, but problems with caste issues relating to the touching of corpses resulted in hundreds of dead remaining in the river. An official estimate placed the actual death toll at around 1000; a figure of around 800 dead certainly seems likely.

UNKNOWN CAUSE

The actual cause of the crash has been difficult to determine. An official report from the Rural Development Minister claimed that sudden braking (possibly caused by a cow on the track) caused the train to derail, but many experts have dismissed this explanation as unlikely. A further explanation came from the Indian Railways Board, which explained that powerful storm winds had simply blown the train from its tracks. Again, many have contested this account, claiming that there would have been prior knowledge of severe weather conditions, which would have stopped the train running in the first place. The mystery of why so many people died in the Bagmati River may never be solved. ■

Above: Many passengers aboard the train would have been killed by the fall from the Samastipur Bridge into the Bagmati, especially as the train was chronically overcrowded. The river was also swollen at the time, and hundreds who managed to escape the carriages were drowned attempting to swim to shore.

Rescue workers scour the waters beneath the Samastipur bridge in the search for survivors. Even today accidents on the Indian rail network average around 300 a year, making it one of the most dangerous rail systems in the world.

BHOPAL

THE BHOPAL DISASTER OF DECEMBER 1984 WAS A MAJOR INDUSTRIAL CATASTROPHE. ACCORDING TO SUBSTANTIATED REPORTS, IT HAS KILLED A TOTAL OF 20,000 PEOPLE TO DATE AND LEFT ANOTHER 120,000 WITH SERIOUS HEALTH PROBLEMS.

The journey to the disaster has its beginnings in the 1970s, when the US-based Union Carbide company established a pesticides factory in the city of Bhopal, India. Owing to the poverty of most of India's farmers, the Bhopal factory ceased to be profitable, and production ceased in the 1980s. However, as the factory contained a mix of highly lethal chemicals, it retained a staff who oversaw storage and safety. All evidence now suggests that the factory was allowed to lapse into disrepair, with corrosion eating into valves, pipes and storage tanks.

DISASTER WAITING TO HAPPEN

On the night of 2/3 December 1984, as an employee was flushing out a rusted pipe, several safety valves ruptured and allowed water to flow into a tank of the chemical methyl isocyanate (MIC). The ingress of water resulted in an explosion in the tank, and an ➤➤

KEY FACTS

2/3 December 1984 – a fractured storage tank at the Union Carbide pesticide plant in Bhopal, India, releases a huge cloud of lethal chemicals over the city.

Up to 15,000 people die in the first week of the disaster, most from asphyxiation and/or damage to the nervous system.

The people of Bhopal continue to suffer from unusually high rates of cancer, respiratory illness, gynaecological disorders, birth defects and blindness.

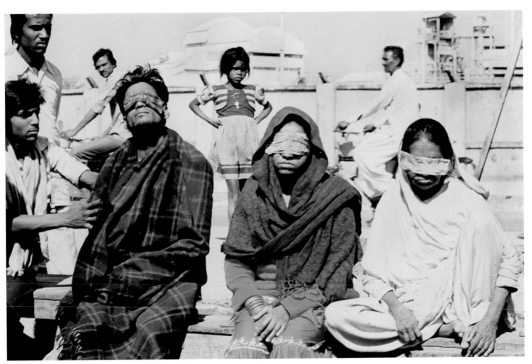

The gases released from the Union Carbide plant were highly aggressive to eye tissue. Thousands of people were completely or partially blinded, and only a lucky few regained their former vision.

Above: Mother Teresa comforts a Bhopal victim. A survivor described the overwhelming effects of the gas: 'It felt like somebody had filled our bodies up with red chillies, our eyes had tears coming out, noses were watering, we had froth in our mouths.'

enormous cloud of lethal MIC gas, and a number of other dangerous chemicals, was released into the air to settle over the densely packed housing of Bhopal.

CHOKING GAS

The effect was horrific. Thousands of people woke with severe choking and asphyxiation. Distraught crowds filled the streets, where bodies were already beginning to pile up. People went blind and died as their lungs filled with fluid, or from convulsions as the chemicals attacked their nervous systems. Estimates for the first week's death toll run from 8000 to 15,000. Yet although the gas dispersed a few days after the initial explosion, people have continued to die in Bhopal from related cancers, respiratory illnesses and brain disorders, and thousands of women have given birth to hideously deformed children. Bhopal is saturated in dangerous substances – levels of mercury in underground water, for example, were found to be up to six million times normal levels. Although the Union Carbide company has paid out $470 million in compensation (very little considering that 500,000 people were exposed), its senior management has effectively escaped criminal prosecution. ∎

Funeral pyres ran constantly in the aftermath of the Bhopal disaster. Corpse disposal became a major problem, as incidences of disease increased. To date, an estimated 20,000 people have died from the initial or long-term effects of the gas.

CHERNOBYL

THE EXPLOSION AT THE CHERNOBYL NUCLEAR POWER PLANT IN THE UKRAINE CHANGED THE WORLD'S RELATIONSHIP TO NUCLEAR POWER.

Chernobyl's first reactor was commissioned in 1977, and the power plant grew to have four reactors in all, producing a total of 3.2 gigawatts of energy.

RADIATION CLOUD

On 26 April 1986, Chernobyl's Reactor No. 4 experienced a catastrophic explosion. The explosion occurred during, ironically, tests for back-up electrical safety systems on the reactors. Mistakes made by the inadequately trained staff resulted in critical overheating, and a huge build-up of steam pressure blew off the reactor's steel and concrete lid, punching a hole through the building's roof. The power plant caught fire and a huge volume of radioactive particles was released into the atmosphere, totalling 30 or 40 times the amount of radiation emitted by the atomic bombs at both Hiroshima and Nagasaki. Radiation was emitted for a total of 10 days, and a radiation cloud spread across ➤➤

Chernobyl as it is today, a desolate Ukrainian wasteland. The city of Pripyat was built in 1977 to house 35,000 citizens, workers and families connected to the plant, but today the site stands almost entirely deserted.

northern Europe – although most of the escaped radiation was concentrated over Belarus, Ukraine and southern Russia.

AMATEUR RESPONSE

A total of 31 people died in the immediate aftermath of the explosion, 28 of those from acute radiation poisoning, and some 200,000 people were evacuated from the surrounding areas and resettled. The Soviet government immediately sent disaster-response teams to Chernobyl, but did not inform most of them of the dangers from radiation or give them adequate safety equipment or protective clothing. A large number would later die of radiation-related cancers. A lack of access to good-quality medical information means that assessing the long-term health damage done by Chernobyl is difficult, yet there has been a distinct rise in certain types of cancers in the worst-exposed areas. In Belarus, for example, children up to the age of 14 experience much higher incidences of thyroid cancer than normal. In total, the Ukraine Radiological Institute has suggested that around 2500 people have died to date from the effects of the Chernobyl disaster. That figure is likely to rise over the next decades. ■

Above: Decontamination work continues today around Chernobyl. Radiation levels in the area remain extremely high, particularly in vegetation such as moss and trees. Children, who are particularly vulnerable to radiation poisoning, were significantly affected.

Chernobyl was abandoned in extreme haste following the explosion. Outside the city perimeter, hundreds of vehicles and numerous military helicopters lie abandoned in fields after they were contaminated during the emergency response.

HILLSBOROUGH DISASTER

ON 15 APRIL 1989, THE HILLSBOROUGH FOOTBALL STADIUM IN THE NORTHERN ENGLISH CITY OF SHEFFIELD, YORKSHIRE, WAS HOST TO A PREMIER FOOTBALLING EVENT, THE FA (FOOTBALL ASSOCIATION) CUP SEMIFINAL BETWEEN NOTTINGHAM FOREST FC AND LIVERPOOL FC.

To manage the threat of football hooliganism – then, unfortunately, a problem common to British football matches – the police had followed the standard practice of separating the rival fans into two different parts of the stadium.

TRAGIC DECISION

The Liverpool supporters were sent to the Leppings Lane end of the stadium, and even before the match began at 3 p.m. there were problems with crowd control. Having travelled some distance on Britain's congested transport system, many of the Liverpool fans were late for the match, and the Leppings Lane turnstiles were overwhelmed by an estimated 5000 late-arriving fans. The police decided to relieve the build-up by opening a set of gates not managed by turnstiles. This decision was to prove disastrous. ➤➤

KEY FACTS

15 April 1989 – Hillsborough football stadium, Sheffield, England, is filled with a capacity crowd for an FA Cup semifinal match.

Police cope with a surge of late arrivals outside the football ground by opening a second gate.

A crush at the Leppings Lane end of the ground results in 96 people dead.

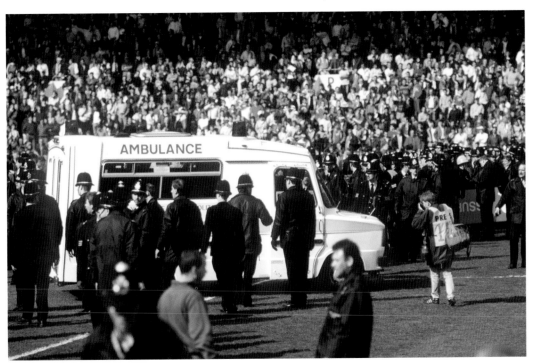

An ambulance moves onto the Hillsborough pitch to treat the injured. A post-disaster report was highly critical of the small numbers of medical personnel available and of the problems the ambulances faced in accessing the ground.

Above: The entire disaster unfolded live on television for the British public, and prompted a wave of national mourning for the victims.

The surge of fans pushing through into the Leppings Lane stands compacted the crowd already standing inside the stadium.

Hundreds of people at the front of the stadium were crushed up against perimeter fencing or against each other, and once the match started the pressure inevitably worsened.

SHOCKING EVENT

At 3.06 p.m., the match was finally stopped; however, by then people were already dead or dying, while dozens more had been injured in the crush. Those spectators that were able to escape climbed over the perimeter fence, or were hoisted up by fans to the terraces above. Some of the pressure was relieved when a small gate in the perimeter fence was finally opened. Both spectators and rescue services attempted to save the lives of as many people as they could, with advertising hoardings being used as improvised stretchers for the victims. The final death toll of the Hillsborough disaster was 96 people, and the whole of the United Kingdom was thrown into a state of shock by the event, which had been televised in its entirety. An independent inquiry into the Hillsborough disaster found that the main causes behind the disaster were overcrowding and the opening of the second gate. ∎

Liverpool players and fans bow their heads for one minute's silence on the fourteenth anniversary of the Hillsborough disaster. The people of Liverpool remain deeply affected by the tragedy, with much anger directed towards the police handling of crowd control.

NEW DELHI AIR DISASTER

DISASTER STRUCK IN THE SKIES SOUTHWEST OF NEW DELHI, INDIA, ON 12 NOVEMBER 1996, WHEN A SAUDI BOEING 747 COLLIDED WITH A KAZAKH ILYUSHIN 76 TRANSPORT FLIGHT, RESULTING IN THE DEATHS OF 351 PEOPLE.

The Saudi airliner, Flight SV763, had taken off from Dharan, Saudi Arabia, and enjoyed a trouble-free flight to New Delhi airport. There, it refuelled for the return journey, taking off at around 6.10 p.m. Inbound for New Delhi, meanwhile, was an Air Kazakhstan charter cargo aircraft, Flight KZA1907, which was nearing the end of its journey from Chiment, Kazakhstan.

A COLLISION COURSE
Air-traffic controllers were aware that the two aircraft were on a potential collision course, so they advised the captains to maintain 328m (1000ft) of altitude between each other, the Saudi aircraft at 4267m (14,000ft) and the Kazakh jet at 4572m (15,000ft).

There is still some confusion over what happened next. The air-traffic controllers confirmed the altitudes with the two pilots; however, it seems that the Kazakh pilot had some problems ➤➤

Debris from the midair collision near New Delhi was scattered for miles over the Indian countryside. In 75 per cent of air crashes, human error rather than mechanical failure is the cause.

understanding the English-language discussion. Furthermore, New Delhi airport did not have the transponder equipment to monitor the aircraft altitudes (radar shows simply flight direction). At 6.14 p.m., however, an air-traffic controller reported that both aircraft had just disappeared from his screen 64km (40 miles) west of New Delhi.

MIDAIR EXPLOSION

Those on the ground at this location reported an enormous aerial explosion, which turned the entire evening sky red. Flaming debris poured from the heavens, thankfully impacting on empty wheat and mustard fields and not inhabited areas. Wreckage from the collision was spread over a large area, that from the Saudi jet being separated by about 10km (6 miles) from the Kazakh wreckage. There were 287 people aboard the Saudi jet and 37 on the Kazakh flight – all were killed. It transpired that the Kazakh jet had for some reason dropped its designated altitude during its final descent, with appalling consequences for both aircraft. ■

Above: A soldier guards a wreckage site. One of the issues to emerge from the disaster was the problem of pilots and air-traffic controllers lacking a common language, and lapsing into their home tongue in a crisis.

Personal belongings litter the crash scene. At the time of the crash, Indian air space had experienced a sevenfold rise in the number of flights in only a few years, without accompanying improvements in safety equipment.

SPACE SHUTTLE *COLUMBIA*

ON 16 JANUARY 2003, THE SPACE SHUTTLE *COLUMBIA* LIFTED OFF FROM HER LAUNCH PAD AT CAPE CANAVERAL WITH SEVEN ASTRONAUTS AND MISSION SPECIALISTS ABOARD, THE FLIGHT COMMANDED BY RICK D. HUSBAND.

By this date, the *Columbia* was the oldest space shuttle in the NASA fleet, having first flown in 1981 (the maiden voyage of the space shuttle programme) and having conducted 26 subsequent missions. Its 2003 mission was entirely scientific, the crew having a busy schedule of 80 experiments to conduct during a 16-day mission, experiments that included research into cancer treatments and zero-gravity firefighting.

SHATTERED TILES

About 81 seconds into launch, several pieces of insulating foam broke off the external fuel tank and struck the left wing of the *Columbia*. Although it is difficult to ascertain what exactly happened at this moment, post-accident reports now conclude that the impact of the foam shattered an area of thermal tiles on the shuttle's wing, the tiles being there to protect the shuttle during ➤➤

KEY FACTS

- **16 January 2003** – *Columbia* is launched on its 28th mission.
- **A piece** of insulating foam breaks off the main fuel tank 81 seconds after launch and damages the heat-resistant tiles on the space shuttle's left wing.
- **1 February** – the *Columbia* disintegrates during re-entry, the damaged left wing allowing catastrophic heat build-up.

A spectacular shuttle launch from Cape Canaveral. The chain of events that led to the Columbia *disaster began just seconds after launch when heat-resistant tiles on the left wing were damaged.*

➦

Above: A poignant memorial to the seven astronauts killed on the Columbia. *Warning sensors in the cockpit would have alerted the crew to the impending disaster some six minutes before the actual break-up of the craft above the United States.*

the 1648°C (3000°F) re-entry temperature. Even the smallest gap in protection would cause catastrophic structural failure.

BREAK-UP

On 1 February 2003, *Columbia* began its re-entry into the earth's atmosphere. At 8.52 a.m. EST, it was crossing over California at a speed of Mach 20.9 and an altitude of more than 67,000m (220,000ft). Shortly afterwards, sensors on the shuttle started to indicate increases in temperature on the left side of the aircraft. The shuttle was due to land at Kennedy Space Center, Florida at 9.16 a.m., but at around 9 a.m. all radio communications between the shuttle and the Space Center were lost. At an altitude of 63,135m (207,135ft), and flying at a speed of 20,116km/h (12,500mph), the *Columbia* disintegrated in flames over East Central Texas, killing all seven crew. Superheated air travelled through a break in the left wing's heat shield and literally melted the wing away, causing loss of flight control and structural break-up. Since the accident, NASA has had to recover from criticisms of its management procedures, identified as a significant factor in the tragedy by an official report, which was careful to take nothing away from the bravery and professionalism of the crew. ■

Accident investigators piece together the remnants of the Columbia *in an aircraft hangar. While the insulating foam that struck the wing would have been too light in itself to do damage, the foam may have accumulated ice to give it weight.*

SEPTEMBER 11 ATTACKS

THE SEPTEMBER 11 ATTACKS STAND AS ONE OF THE MOST IMPORTANT WORLD EVENTS OF THE TWENTY-FIRST CENTURY.

The tragedy began on the morning of 11 September 2001. A total of 19 terrorists, all connected to the Islamic group al-Qaeda, boarded four commercial airliners, two flying out of Boston, one from Washington DC and the fourth from Newark, New Jersey. Once the aircraft were airborne, the hijackers took them over and seated themselves at the controls. (Some of the terrorists had undergone flight training in United States.)

DEVASTATING ATTACK

At 8.46 a.m. (local time), American Airlines Flight 11 was flown into the north tower of the World Trade Center in New York City. Fully fuelled, the aircraft exploded in an enormous fireball and set the upper floors of the building ablaze. This was just the beginning. At 9.03 a.m., United Airlines Flight 175 struck the south tower; at 9.37 a.m., the Pentagon in Washington DC was struck by American Airlines Flight 77; and finally, around 10.20 a.m., United Airlines Flight 93 crashed in a field in Pennsylvania. ➤➤

KEY FACTS

- **11 September 2001** – four US airlines on domestic flights are hijacked. Two planes are flown into the World Trade Center, one into the Pentagon and another crashes in Pennsylvania.
- **The World Trade Center** towers collapse, killing nearly 1800 people.
- **The total** death toll comes to nearly 3000, and the events are the catalyst for a major US anti-terrorism campaign.

The south tower of the World Trade Center is hit by the second hijacked aircraft, while the north tower burns.

By far the greatest death toll of that terrible day occurred in New York City. The intense heat of the fires caused the World Trade Center's south tower to collapse at 9.59 a.m., and the north tower also collapsed half an hour later. These two incidents cost the lives of 2800 people, including around 400 police officers and firefighters and 157 people on the aircraft. In the Pentagon, 189 people were killed, and all 45 people aboard Flight 93 in Pennsylvania also died. The final death toll rose to 2986, more than the total number of people who were killed at Pearl Harbor in 1941.

Above: The fully loaded fuel tanks of the two airliners that crashed into the towers meant that there was enough heat in the fires to melt the structural steelwork.

WAR AGAINST TERRORISM

The September 11 attacks have had a profound effect on the United States and the world in general. Under President George Bush, the United States began a massive, and politically controversial, global anti-terrorism operation. The United States and Allied nations subsequently went to war in Afghanistan and overthrew the ruling Taliban regime. Soon after the September 11 attacks there were terrorist attacks in Madrid and Bali which are also said to be the work of al-Qaeda. ∎

Rescue workers stand in silent remembrance at Ground Zero. Up to 10,000 children in New York City lost one or both of their parents in the World Trade Center attacks.

IRANIAN EARTHQUAKE

THE 2000-YEAR-OLD CITY OF BAM WAS, AND REMAINS, A TRULY UNIQUE URBAN AREA.

During the Early Modern period, Bam was a prosperous trading centre situated on the Silk Road between East Asia and the Mediterranean, and was also a place of faith and pilgrimage. At its heart is the ancient citadel of Arg-e-Bam, much of it dating back to the Safavid dynasty (1501–1736) and built mainly out of mud brick and clay straw. Despite the passage of time, much of the more recent housing in Bam was constructed along similar lines. A typical Bam house featured a mud-brick outer shell, capped by a heavy concrete and steel-girder roof. Often, to increase size of the living quarters, more internal floors were added than was structurally safe.

DEVASTATING EARTHQUAKE

Within this fragile city, about 142,000 people were living. At 5.26 a.m. on 26 December 2003, an earthquake with a magnitude of 6.5 struck Kermam province, with the epicentre only 10km (6 miles) southwest of Bam city. The earthquake shook for only ➤➤

KEY FACTS

26 December 2003 – an earthquake of 6.5 magnitude demolishes 80 per cent of the historic city of Bam, Kermam province, Iran.

The devastation is increased by the prevalence of poor quality mud-brick housing in the city.

The final death toll reaches more than 26,000.

The destruction in Bam was total, particularly as the poverty of many of its inhabitants meant that their homes were constructed of little more than wood-framed mud brick.

Above: Rescue workers attempt to find survivors of the Bam earthquake. Isolated survivors were found buried in the rubble two weeks after the disaster.

around 12 seconds, but in that short space of time 80 per cent of Bam collapsed, killing thousands of people instantly, the death toll increased by the fact that many people were asleep at the time of the earthquake and so were unable to respond effectively. The mud-brick houses, so evocative to look at, had almost no earthquake resistance and simply folded in on themselves.

DEVASTATED CITY

The devastation was total. When interviewed shortly after the disaster, Iranian Interior Minister Abdolvahed Mousavi Lari said, 'Bam has turned into a wasteland. Even if a few buildings are standing, you cannot trust to live in them.' Several days after the earthquake occurred, international aid began to arrive in substantial quantities, yet by that time a total of 26,271 people were dead, many of them asphyxiated in the rubble of their collapsed housing. Another 120,000 people were homeless, with estimated rebuilding costs placed at $1 billion. Iranian authorities claimed that the rebuilding of the city would include more earthquake-resistant constructions, although only time will tell whether the promise is fulfilled. ∎

The initial death toll from the Bam disaster was placed in the region of 41,000 people. However, it was discovered that there had been some errors in counting the fatalities, with some of the dead being counted twice.

INDIAN OCEAN TSUNAMI

ON 26 DECEMBER 2004, AN UNDERWATER EARTHQUAKE OCCURRED IN THE INDIAN OCEAN.

It was a huge seismic event, scientists estimating that it measured 9 on the Richter scale – the highest level of destructive force. The incredible release of energy even caused the earth to wobble on its axis. The earthquake literally ruptured the sea floor along the juncture of the Australian and Eurasian tectonic plates, causing the sea floor to shift upwards by several metres and in turn triggering a huge tsunami, which radiated out across the Indian Ocean.

OCEANWIDE DESTRUCTION

Travelling at speeds of up to 800km/h (500mph), but slowing and rising to a height of 10–15m (32–50ft) near land, the wave first hit the western Indonesia coastline, the closest destination to the epicentre of the earthquake. The resulting devastation was total, the wave sweeping away thousands of people and wiping entire coastal regions off the face of the map. This happened within 15 minutes of the earthquake, but the tsunami went on to cause death and destruction across the Indian Ocean over the next seven hours, wrecking coastlines as far distant as Somalia, some 7241km (4500 miles) away. ➤➤

KEY FACTS

- **26 December 2004** – an earthquake measuring 9 on the Richter scale occurs in the Indian Ocean around 160km (100 miles) northwest of Sumatra.
- **The earthquake** triggers a tsunami, which devastates communities as far away as 7240km (4500 miles) from the epicentre.
- **Current figures** place the death toll around 150,000, with the possibility of climbing to 300,000.

The tsunami races into shore as individuals in the surf fruitlessly run to escape the waters.

By the end of 26 December, it was becoming clear that the tsunami had caused one of the greatest aquatic disasters in history. At the time of writing, more than 150,000 people have been confirmed dead, and that toll is expected to rise. Indonesia was the worst hit, Sumatra being only 160km (100 miles) from the epicentre, and it lost 94,000-plus people; Sri Lanka lost around 30,500; southeastern India, nearly 9000; Thailand, 6000 people; and other countries affected include Bangladesh, Myanmar, Malaysia, the Maldives and Somalia.

Disaster response

The tsunami disaster has generated an enormous worldwide aid response. As we have seen in many examples throughout this book, the initial disaster may be just the beginning of the problem, and subsequent deaths from disease and malnutrition can far exceed those killed by the initial event itself (currently around 1.5 million people are homeless). Today's international community has infinitely better medical and aid responses than the world had even 50 years ago, and we can only hope that new technology and medicines will prevent the scale of the disaster becoming any worse than it already is. ■

Above: Helicopter became the only viable method of reaching people in the most inundated areas. A typical air lift by a Sea King helicopter could deliver enough food to feed 727 people for a total of 30 days.

The earthquake under the Indian Ocean in December 2004 awakened the world to the full power of a tsunami. Coastlines bordering the ocean were turned into wildernesses, with many areas inaccessible to international rescue services.

INDEX